On the Universal

On the Universal, the uniform, the common and dialogue between cultures

FRANÇOIS JULLIEN

Translated by

MICHAEL RICHARDSON AND KRZYSZTOF FIJALKOWSKI

polity

First published in French as *De l'universel, de l'uniforme, du commun et du dialogue entre les cultures* © Librairie Arthème Fayard, 2008

This English edition © Polity Press, 2014

This book is supported by the Institut français (Royaume-Uni) as part of the Burgess programme (www.frenchbooknews.com)

Polity Press
65 Bridge Street
Cambridge CB2 1UR, UK

Polity Press
350 Main Street
Malden, MA 02148, USA

ISBN-13: 978-0-7456-4622-0
ISBN-13: 978-0-7456-4623-7(pb)

A catalogue record for this book is available from the British Library.

Typeset in 11.5 on 14 pt Fournier by
Servis Filmsetting Ltd, Stockport, Cheshire
Printed and bound in Great Britain by Clays Ltd, St Ives plc

The publisher has used its best endeavours to ensure that the URLs for external websites referred to in this book are correct and active at the time of going to press. However, the publisher has no responsibility for the websites and can make no guarantee that a site will remain live or that the content is or will remain appropriate.

Every effort has been made to trace all copyright holders, but if any have been inadvertently overlooked the publisher will be pleased to include any necessary credits in any subsequent reprint or edition.

For further information on Polity, visit our website: www.politybooks.com

To Léon Vandermeersch with thanks for his keen support.
To Arnold Davidson, Du Xiaozhen, Roberto Esposito, Paolo Fabbri,
Peter Gente, Wolfgang Kubin, Le Huu Khoa, Lin Chi-ming for the
understanding we achieved at a distance.

The translators would like to thank Robin Weichart, Liliana Albertazzi
and François Jullien for their help, and Leigh Mueller for her sterling
copy-editing.

Contents

Foreword

In various corners of the world, in the midst of exchanges and traffic of every type (of both people and goods), and even during wars and deportations, cultures are still somewhere undoubtedly (irreducibly) committed to dialogue with one another. Obliquely, to the point of extinction, in a stubborn way: through borrowings, contaminations and influences, but also through misunderstandings, resistances, twistings, dissidences, or simply through the traces and testimony buried beneath the ruins uncovered by History. Even so, it is only remarkably recently that the question of dialogues between cultures has been made explicit. No doubt, the relation between cultures had to change in both scale and regime (and it did so in a brutal way) before this question could be posed: starting with simple sporadic relations due to proximity, the resulting relationships had to assume a global dimension and, thanks to the meticulous work of anthropologists, the cultural inventory of a finite world might appear close to completion. Moreover, the culture that has become dominant over these past centuries (the 'Western' one) has been forced to recognize that its sovereign position is being chipped away and it can no longer assert its pre-established legitimacy so dogmatically. Today this leads to a contrasting and largely contradictory situation: on the one hand, there is standardization in lifestyles, production, consumption and a mediatization which, the world over, threatens to envelop all cultural diversity (to such an extent that it becomes obscured), and, on the other hand, conflicts of a cultural order that, far from fading away, become more virulent, thanks to the ideological form they now adopt as they take up the baton of the old imperialisms, whose explosive charge resounds both here and there. However you look at it, the conditions for an *intelligent* dialogue, between cultures, are far from being assured.

What has brought us to this impasse? Why does such a 'dialogue' weary us from the outset, even though we know it is indispensable? Isn't it precisely because it is today still too strongly steeped in good intentions, and because it has not been constructed well enough for it to be ultimately credible? What I mean is that the overly *ideologically correct* character surrounding it may induce public indifference, in spite of the proofs and denials attached to it. So, I believe the only way we will be able to extract it from the sloppy humanism in which it is bathed, but which is also its undoing, is methodically to reduce it to its essentials for discussion. This is why, in order to revive the question, I intend to set off from three closely related terms (those of the universal, the uniform and the common) which form a triangle, but which we have too often either confused with one another or considered separately. These three notions obviously intersect but at different levels. Likewise, while the prevailing discourse is content to consider them equivalent, or at least pretends to do so, or else pursues one of them alone without adjusting it to the others, my approach will be the opposite: at once to probe their divergence and to conceive them in relation, and to do so with a view to raising the table of future debates on this tripod. I will therefore start by considering them in turn, but will do so in order to allow myself to fine-tune their inter-relationship. Still, it is a good idea first to scrape them clean so their plain forms can be recovered from out of the mire into which *doxa* has cast them. In fact, let's be brave enough to hoist the discussion up from the slackness of opinion, carving it out from the concept.

Note on the text

This text has been developed from a talk given within the framework of the methodical and popular philosophy course organized by the Institute of Contemporary Thought at University Paris-7 Denis Diderot in collaboration with the Mairie de Paris (10 May 2006).

I believe genre should be used properly. The text that follows arises from that of Discourse or Letters; it advances speedily by accumulating references to make the question posed intelligible. Do we not indeed need to set to with an axe if we are to hack out a path through what the immensity of knowledge required has rendered inaccessible and that the regime of public opinion has carefully kept so entangled as to be impenetrable?

Since I had been attacked by strident defenders of a sloppy humanism, the time had come for me to comment on the question of the universal. But the only way I can do it is to construct a triangle – one which places the universal in tension, both with the uniform (its opposite) and with the common (which it inspires).

Wasn't the 'dialogue between cultures' itself to be extracted from this reign of slipshod thought?

Itinerary

I Critique of notions – chapters I to III

If we wish to think about the relationships between cultures, what notions do we have at our disposal that are able to be effectively promoted conceptually? Aren't they all impaired and subject to criticism from at least one side? Even the *universal*, a rigorous concept of reason and one derived from the theory of knowledge, cannot hide its ambiguity: does it simply serve as a recognition of a totality acknowledged in experience, or does it name an imperative to be projected *a priori* and in so doing establish an absolute norm for the whole of humanity? As soon as one considers the singular history – contradicting what it demands – from which it was born, in its desperate conflict with the singular, something repeated at each new phase of philosophy, one can no more believe in the transparency of this notion than in the neutrality of its use.

Then, far from being its comforting realization, the *uniform* is the perverted double of that universal which is now being spread by globalization. As it saturates the world, it surreptitiously masquerades as the universal without being able to invoke legitimacy. It is authorised not by necessity but by convenience, arising from an interest not of reason but of production, and by indefinitely diffusing the similar it turns it into the only landscape we have and so gives it accreditation. Thus its dictatorship is all the more insidious for being discreet and for not bringing attention to itself.

As for the *common*, it is really the place where things are shared and, as such, it is directly political. Unlike the universal, it does not invoke a hypothetical *a priori* but shows up the groundless ground in which our experience is rooted and to whose deployment it contributes. Thus it extends indefinitely. Despite this, it is always threatened by reversal: from being inclusive, to becoming exclusive. Instead of opening out onto more participation, it may tip into its opposite: 'communitarianism'.[1]

II European genealogy – chapters IV to VII

Nevertheless, by following the thread of history, from the time that the City State emerges we see the common being effectively deployed until it encounters the demand for the universal that is at the heart of Stoic cosmopolitanism. But, as it guided this extension of the common, the universal was not as unified with it as was believed. For the universal is composed of various levels at the heart of European culture. These are logical (with the arrival of the concept); juridical (with the institution of Roman citizenship); and religious (with the Pauline dissolution of all cleavage in divine love and the economy of salvation).

Contrary to what it stands for in philosophy, doesn't the universal therefore arise from a composite – not to say chaotic – arrangement? And doesn't its prestige stem, in Europe, from what it contributes towards binding all of this heterogeneity within it while serving as its ideological keystone?

III Enquiry and problematization – chapters VIII to XI

Hence the necessity for philosophy finally to emerge from what it is comfortable with, even if it has to change regime, to undertake explorations and break with its securitized order of reasons. What is the notion of the universal worth once the European frame has been abandoned, and, above all, can it remain intelligible within it? This question is itself broken into two parts: (1) to what extent have other cultures developed such a demand? and (2) are there any notions which from the outset, that is *a priori*, might be considered universal? That we cannot be certain of responding affirmatively to either of these questions forces us to think about the validity of the universal afresh, to conceive of it no longer as a positive and saturated totality but, inversely, as the exigency inherent to the *negative* of opening up any closed and self-satisfied universality – precisely what enables universalism to prevail.

Equally, from that point on it will no longer be possible to understand the *commonality* [*commun*] of cultures as either a synthesis, a denominator or a foundation, but as the common of the *intelligible*, in continual deployment and guided by this 'regulating' universal. Human rights are a privileged example of this. The West can no longer claim to export them for their positive content, arrogantly teaching others how to live, when their negative side, by causing an *a priori* of refusal to loom up in the face of what their failure suddenly reveals as unconditionally unacceptable (i.e. independently of perspectives inherent to various cultures), stands as an efficient and not yet blunted *universalizing* force.

IV Stakes and positions – chapters XII to XIII

The result of this is first of all that the plurality of cultures is no longer to be considered in terms of an inventorying of difference, but of the exploration of the *divergence* which sets up a tension, revealing the extent of the possibilities and disclosing the diversity of cultures as so many *resources* to exploit. This is a way to invite a move away from a sterile defence of cultural identity towards the fertility that begins with resistance to the uniformization that globalization has engendered. A 'dia-logue' of cultures will itself have force only if it brings into play this *dia* of the divergence and the negative at the same time as it allows itself to be situated on this single common level of the *intelligible* (*logos*). Through the device it establishes as it erects the various cultures in relation to one another and by no longer assuming a universality that is given from the outset, it produces the new conditions for a *self-reflection of the human* – the infinite work in progress henceforth disclosed once the last mythologies of Man have been devastated.

I On the universal

1 Let us therefore begin abruptly and *sharply*, at the top of the triangle, the most prominent of the three corners. The universal issues an injunction which even haunts debate and the sort of blandness that has become common, for the imperative and even imperious justification it invokes functions according to law and is not simply a matter of fact. In spite of all that actually dulls its edges at the heart of ordinary language and verbal sparring, it is hard to see how we can maintain any doubt about its identity. The universal declares itself to be a concept of reason and, as such, it lays claim to a necessity formed *a priori* – in other words, one that is prior to any experience. At least this is what it is in its strictest sense and is what makes it a threshold through which philosophy is entered. This requirement immediately leads us to distinguish between two modes, or rather two levels, of 'universality'. On the one hand, we see a weak universality, one that is closed, languid and limited to experience alone and which, to avoid running into the sharpness of the concept, would like to content itself with standard usage, without making clear its relation to its other form. This means that we record the fact that, in so far as we have until now been able to observe it, such a thing always occurs in this way, or that it concerns every case (of the same class). On the other hand, we see a strong universality, a strict or rigorous universality, which philosophy has conceived and considers as the only legitimate form: we assert from the outset, before any confirmation has been given by experience, that such a thing *must* occur in this way. There is no possible exception to this: we affirm not only that until the present day such a thing has always *existed* in this way, but that it *cannot* be otherwise. The two terms are reciprocal, in fact, and they coincide: only properly necessary judgements can strictly be universal (as also only strictly universal judgements can be absolutely necessary).

Any prior watering down is fruitless: from the outset the universal compels this unhooking and absolutization. Or, to express this with still greater clarity (because reason's intransigence is never even slightly negotiable), while persevering with the Kantian terms with which we started: the first of these judgements is merely extensive, but the second is imperative. The former merely exists as such and is limited to experience, being nothing but a general judgement, while the latter, existing in law, is strictly 'universal' (*allgemein*). In other words, only what is necessary *a priori* can be universal as a law. Or the first is universal only relatively or 'comparatively', while the second is so 'absolutely'. The complete extension of the latter, in relation to the condition granted, comes neither from a progressive totalization, nor even from an indefinitely repeated observation (i.e. a never-contradicted attribution), but really from a *prescription* posed as a pre-established principle and having a value as law. In this it is really a pure expression of Reason, and serves it as an exigency.

I admit that this approach is difficult and chilling, allowing of no further faltering, and it breaks with the blandness that surrounds it. It is nevertheless necessary for me to begin at this point, above this sheer drop, setting myself up at the top of the cliff, which is where European Reason has perched us: on the founding rock of reason that overhangs and totally dominates the waves in everlasting eddies (an old image underlying metaphysics, which is very difficult to banish) which are those of human restlessness and development, of the reigns of 'opinion' and 'experience'. Indeed, to begin with, I cannot emphasize too much the non-empirical, non-stated but *decreed* character of logical necessity (in short, the deliberated dismantling of every given, that sudden leap from the regime of the relative to that of the absolute) by which classical European philosophy defined the judgement of universality from the outset. For when the universal is discussed today in the dialogue between cultures, we can no longer pretend that we have forgotten the precise place, epistemologically and culturally circumscribed as it is, from which its need was introduced: from the 'evidence' of science, of course, for which only knowledge governed by concepts of understanding (deduced transcendentally as 'categories') is objective, is therefore necessarily applicable always and for everyone, does not vary from one case to another, is cleansed of all subjectivity and, as such, is universally valid (the type of knowledge from which Kant deduced precisely the conditions of possibility in his *Critique of Pure Reason*). Actually, these conditions have formed us so effectively and been so well assimilated by us, and then we have so capably exported them to the rest of the world ('we' meaning those we conveniently term 'Westerners') that, by evoking them in such an abrupt way, I may be giving the tedious impression of reiteration.

What could actually be more thankless than to begin by once more going back over this catechism of reason, if all it does is reshape the anticipated and even inevitable question around which our debates endlessly turn? Is such a universality (one modelled upon mathematical proof and resting on necessary and formal liaison alone, operating *a priori* in the mind, independently of everything we could learn through observation or personal experience, but whose validation, from the perspective of science, is incontestable – within a few centuries, through its physical applications, it has really changed the face of our planet) still so applicable when we are no longer dealing with the knowledge we construct of things but return to the human? In other words, does it apply when the liaison at issue is concerned with the relation of subjects rather than with objective truth, or when we go from the laws of science to those of values, or from science's conditions of possibility to those of ethics and politics? The issue can be summed up by returning precisely to what now becomes the problem: between cultures, can (and must) we today envisage *living in common* under the demands of a pre-established universality and by means of its enlightenment?

For example, when we consult the Universal Declaration of Human Rights, which here functions as a Manifesto, we can see very well that 'universal' cannot simply signify in a weak way but extends over the whole surface of the Earth and for this reason concerns all peoples and all countries (as we speak of a 'Universal Exhibition', or a universal geography or history). And this is so even if technological development over the past century, with the ending of the great explorations and under the pressure of colonialism, has meant that the history of the 'finite world' has started and that the globe has been traversed in every direction: that all territories, starting with the European epicentre, have been systematically accessed and gone over with a fine-toothed comb, so that the 'human family', to which such a Declaration is addressed, is finally complete. Here 'universal' denotes not simply this maximal extension, of an empirical nature (in short, some sort of planetarization), but really implies a prescription. At least it suggests that a strong universality, founded on a necessity pre-established as a principle, therefore being of a logical nature, justifies its conception, even if, as has often been noted,[1] the ambiguity of the text in this respect has not been entirely removed. Unease arises at this point, because such a Declaration contains within itself, even if only through the attribution of legitimacy given by 'declaring', the invocation of an imperative [*devoir-être*].[2]

2 Kant himself at least had the merit of not indulging ambiguity: the exigency of universality (universality in the strong sense: of right) will apply to morality as much as to knowledge. This exclusive command will leave no place for the diversity of cultures – in truth the question did not arise for Kant, or rather he had no idea that it existed. For him, a cultural self (a subject) did not exist, all human behaviour being subject as a principle to the same law, which was conceived from the universality inherent to the *laws of nature*, whose logical necessity science had finally discovered. Hence this imperative, being universal, could only be exclusive (according to the well-known motto, 'act only on that maxim whereby you can at the same time will that it should become a universal law': Kant, 1969: 45). Before undertaking an action, 'I' – in other words *any* human subject, independently of any condition, including cultural ones – will ask itself only this: can I universalize the maxim of this act? If I wish to test its morality, all I have to do is mentally to convert the principle which inspires it into a 'universal law of nature' so that I may deduce its consequences.

This is really the basic postulate that, in the form of a more or less latent Kantianism, has constantly underlain European consciousness: in each case, whether we are talking about action or knowledge, about my relation to others or about knowledge of objects, only a universality that is installed before the event into all experience can provide *legitimacy*. Under this exclusive exigency of reason, which even constitutes 'reason' as such, we see the two levels completely matched, or more precisely one lies beneath the other: action *below* knowledge, behaviour *below* the theoretical. The same legislatory activity reigns on both sides, over 'nature' just as much as over 'will', over 'necessity' just as much as over 'freedom' – from the outset, such categories are valid for humanity as a whole. As I say, it never occurred to Kant that they arose from a singular history of thought. Consequently his conception became impermeable and unflinchingly developed this unique exigency of reason – indeed, as what constitutes reason – probably taking it as far as anyone will ever take it. The independence will in fact be the same for action as for knowledge, since it imposes on both of them an equal imperative [*devoir-être*] regarding any given encountered (precisely that which the contingency of our motives and inclinations manifests in the moral sphere). And, likewise, there will be the same 'objectivity' on both sides (in morality, by abandoning the 'for us', sacrificed to benefit humanity's 'ends in themselves'). In short, the same 'formal' character is found even in behaviour and it arises from a pure logical deduction. Proof of this lies in the fact that the only 'flaw' envisaged affecting action and morality is also that purely *formal* flaw which is contradiction: will the universalization of the maxim of my act contradict the universal law of nature or, at the very least, that of the 'essence of my will'?

The question of the universal, as it arises between cultures, therefore emerges from its ideological haze thanks to this Kantian radicalization whose demand leads action systematically to fold back onto the probing model of knowledge, even if I have to admit that the sudden illumination it casts is of a lunar pallor As a principle this universal will transcend any difference between cultures, since it is applied not only to people but equally – according to the unprecedented extrapolation from which Kant began – to all rational beings that might understand, not only in the world but 'even in general outside of the world' (Kant, 1969). Can a formulation more grandiloquent in its extension and peremptory in its affirmation be conceived (or imagined)? Or one that extends the original scene of its validity more disproportionately (or abruptly)? But let's dispel the mirage: isn't the form of reason with which this requirement made by universality is confused, and which establishes its foundation, the singular product of European intellectual history alone, trained as it is on the demands that Truth makes, and even perhaps obsessed by them? And, above all, absolutized as it is as a supreme attribute at the very heart of European thought, shouldn't the universal also properly be considered as what it is: a pure *attribute* and, as such, not essential but simply 'accidental'? The term as well as the question is already to be found in Aristotle.

3 Whether we elevate ourselves from what is presently perceived to the physical law which explains it, or whether we wonder about the possible universalization of the maxim of our action, thus allowing it also to be erected into a natural law, the universality that has been demanded, in order to arrive at the imperative [*devoir-être*], always ensues from that process which philosophy has tamed so effectively – precisely what has forever detached it from 'wisdom' and set it upon its singular destiny: that of 'abstraction'. Abstraction, at the very heart of European thought, is therefore what wisdom finally has to be judged by. If the universal is to be attained, one always has to start by elevating oneself beyond any one example, by overstepping the limits of this thing or that action, by not dwelling in the immediacy to which I am committed (that *here* and *now* constituting my attachment). When considered globally through its history, but also in comparison to the thought of other cultures, we see that European philosophy owes its astonishing escalation, or the possibility of its development, to its extension between the two poles it has constituted as boundary points: the universal, when it erected its 'logic', that of *logos*, established the ineffable *concrete* (of enjoyment or sensation) as its exact opposite. After this, can we fail to wonder whether European thought is alone in being so torn? Consequently, would it alone find itself cast into a history determined, through despair and reversal, by the effort needed to emerge from this contradiction? For, if the universal is dissociated from the 'here' and 'now', these are also revealed (through a reversal, by means of indicating other places and other moments) to be the most universal, but because of this the most abstract and therefore equally the most empty terms that could exist, as Hegel had already noted was the outcome of this invention of Reason. This was on the threshold of his *Phenomenology* (do we need to be reminded that this was a 'phenomenology' only of the European 'mind'?), when he dreamt precisely of effecting the reconciliation of the 'universal' and the 'concrete' through a dialectical sublation and total development of the *logos*, which was expected to provide the salvation that would finally bring down the curtain on the drama.

Indeed, there really is a European drama of thought since, at the heart of the 'concrete', the universal is opposed by forms such as the *individual* or the *singular* which do not concede anything to the demands it makes. It is therefore also pertinent to start by questioning it from this opposition. The first stage of philosophy: as European thought is articulated in the word 'Being', the question it has continually developed as an alternative, in its ancient and medieval periods, could only lead to the conjecture of whether it is the universal *or* the individual which actually 'exists'. This is an old debate that has remained open (or rather has been impossible to resolve?): do these abstract universals which reason elaborates really exist in the world (and not just in the mind, which is the 'realist' position) or are they simply nominal entities, meaning that only the individual exists (the 'nominalist' position)? The debate took its point of departure with the divorce from Platonism effected by Aristotle, but it is one whose history, beyond reductionist slogans, has very much continued to pass through various reconfigurations, none of which are definitive (see Libera, 1996). Was this examination, which appears obviously necessary to us, therefore without an outcome from the start? Having *passed it by*, wouldn't the thought of other cultures teach us that, enfolded in this choice of Being as it is, European thought can consequently be justified only by itself?

Or else, by heroically conquering all of its classical predicates (predicates which are closely related: the formal, the necessary, the objective and so on), the universal would inevitably encounter the resistance of a new figure in its path, the subjective of *pure singularity*, in modern philosophy (or rather in its anti-philosophy, between Nietzsche and Kierkegaard, which no longer thinks about the existence of things conjointly with the order of the world, but rather about the intransigence and incommensurability of the Subject). Or would this once again open up a fresh fault-line (or an infinitely fertile fissure) in which European thought alone would find what it actually needed to promote its 'modernity'? Contrary to all the gregarious universalisms which have led to nihilism, to be 'individual' becomes as far as possible the final and greatest challenge. Fidelity to its appeal is the only exigency because human truth is moored to nothing but this singularity. From that viewpoint, universalization appears as the great facility-facticity. The demand it imposes is a violence done to *existence*, which means that it is what thought must rebel against. 'He was the Individual' was what Kierkegaard wished to have on his tomb.

This turnaround is admittedly hackneyed, banal to consider, and tiresome to repeat, but it remains a matter of concern to us (would it even be possible to rid ourselves of it?). With its ideal ambition (of reason), the universal finds itself accused here of falsification (in relation to experience), in other words of treason (in relation to the very demand made by truth). From one age to the next, the staging of the trial has been transformed, but today we do not suspect it of hegemony, let alone of a hidden reign of terror, one that is even more dangerous in that it is presented as being impeccably 'pure' and as having logic on its side. If its concept is effectively clear because it is engendered according to what is required by reason, its status remains at the very least ambiguous and it is threatened with delusion. Can anyone really believe in the transparency of the universal, or even regard it simply as a neutral tool? Or if, at the level erected by the discourse – *logos* – within which it sits so comfortably (since this is what belongs to it), it easily rids itself (that is, in a Hegelian way) of its adversaries (the unthinkable Concrete, the silent Singularity, the evasive Intuition, and so on), and feels able to progress straight to the Absolute, we begin to think that it is perhaps simply because it operates *without constraint*, without anything further fastening on to it. And, above all, now that we are starting to learn from those who are not indigenous to Europe, can we continue to avoid asking the question of whether this 'universal' can be so easily (universally) expressed in all languages? And by doing so, we will be better able to reveal (in a way that neither Kant nor Hegel could imagine) that we think *in language*.

Hence this third and current stage, of rebellion against the universal, in which the singularity – no longer of the Substance (as in Antiquity), or of the Subject (as in modern philosophy), but of the Other of other cultures (in the 'postmodern' age, of which this is one of the arguments) – is defended. Since it is easy to observe that the universal is something in which other cultures have shown hardly any interest, to the extent that often they do not even have a name for it, their rebellion in this respect cannot be truly expressed other than precisely by using this European term which has been imposed on them and which they have needed to translate. Consequently, they have once again had to express it through the mouth of the Other and so once more they betray themselves. Its murmuring is nonetheless heard from then on as soon as it is referred to, and we are unable to escape its ambient effect. Doesn't such a universal in fact consecrate the currently shaky and so all the more unmanageable supremacy of Western reason as well as the imperialism of the civilization underlying it? Hasn't this turned it into just another slogan? This debate, which might have been expected to be quickly exhausted, is actually, I believe, only just beginning. But, before getting involved in it, we will need to support it by returning to what we should really call the Greek *branch* of thought and, more precisely, to the way in which the universal is still dependent upon the concept. Is it even slightly possible to dissociate the universal, and the absolute which inhabits it, from the very choice of philosophy? If it is, then philosophy would be revealed, in contradiction with the requirement underlying the universal that has carried it along, to be an adventure singular to thought alone.

II On the uniform

1 It is certainly rather audacious to claim to make such a frontal and summary attack on these notions. But the ways in which each of them illuminates the others will soon become apparent due to the tensions they set up. Today the world seems to be confused between the universal and the uniform. It appears to be readily accepted that the uniform serves only to duplicate and reinforce the universal, that it does no more than prolong its effects and make them manifest. I believe the reverse to be the case, and that this opposition, in the age of globalization, has become crucial. Let's go back to the guiding principles of these notions. While the universal is 'turned' towards the One (*uni-versus*) and expresses an aspiration towards it, the uniform is only a sterile repetition of this One. In truth the nature of this 'one' has itself, without warning, completely toppled from universal to uniform. The latter is no longer the eminent and transcendent (Plotinian) One, to which the mind is converted in order to escape from the fragmentation of the diverse (of the *di-versus*), but the reduced, completely deadened and arid one, of consistent regularity and seriality. Instead of ideally (and vertically) bringing about a convergence towards the absolute of a principle, it is no more than the indefinite return of the same and, unlike the universal, spreads out all the more easily (and prolifically) because it is not concerned about its foundation. This is significant today now that the universal is being turned around, right under our noses, for the convenience of the uniform. Indeed, by successfully masquerading as the universal, the uniform secretly becomes the perversion of it.

This is why we openly separate the two: the uniformity of ways of life, discourse and opinions that now tend to span the globe from one end to the other thanks to technology and the media does not, for all that, mean that they are universal. Even if they are to be found absolutely everywhere, to the point of saturating everything, they always lack an imperative [*devoir-être*]. In fact this disjunction of levels operates prior to the slippage from the universal to the uniform. The opposition between them could be summed up as follows: the uniform is a concept of production (such as the standard or the stereotype), not of reason. It arises not from a necessity but from convenience: it is less costly because it is produced on an assembly line. Its only merit is to increase the yield and make every-thing easier. Even in the most favourable case – that of a standardization of measures, codes and jurisdictions – it is the principle of functionality alone that prevails in it. Moreover, it is not even certain that the equality which would result from such standardization, in the domain of law or education for example, would be anything more than a false covering. This could be expressed in another way: the only rationality with which the uniform could be credited is principally to do with economics and management; it rests on imitation and is not, in any event – in contrast to the universal – of the order of logic and the prescriptive.

As it unhooks itself from experience to appeal to the imperative [*devoir-être*], the universal ostensibly arouses rebellion – that of the singularity of the one that is 'here and now', whether of the individual Subject or of the inalienable Other. In contrast, the uniform, in its pandemic quality, is content to deaden any resistance towards it and blend into the landscape; it is carried along by *habitus* and is authorized only by its frequency. Its power, in other words, is simply cumulative: the more widely it is spread, the more it imposes itself and the more it spreads, and so on. Consequently, if it were to be considered as such – in other words as an indefinite extension of the similar – it would not be possible to prove, or even simply to find, pertinence in it, and it would therefore have no further need to legitimate itself; nothing is hooked on to it or is even noticeable about it. Moreover, to pause for just a moment over this 'similar' on which it is supported, we find also that it is a poor concept, one that defers its justification over the other and consequently is no better able to set up anything: it is a superficial concept because it is purely aspectual. It is content to reflect the image, and lacks even the totalizing rigour of the generic. Even the well-known 'brotherly love' doesn't mean anything.

2 Our resources will therefore be found rather on the flip-side of the uniform. As what is opposite to the universal is the individual or the singular, so the opposite of the uniform is the *different*. Difference rather than resemblance is the motivating concept and it is fertile because of

its negative nature. Whereas the uniform blurs and *deadens* by means of its regularities, going as far as to cause a loss of awareness of the thing, difference creates tension, highlights, promotes and shapes. The initial *dis-* (or *dia-*) expresses the divergence which 'carries along', and what, because of this, due to this divergence, 'is important' (*diapherei*, in Greek: 'it is important that . . .'). It is through the statement of difference, Aristotle tells us, that we respond to the 'what is it?' at the level of knowledge, which coincides for the Greeks with that of definition, *logos*. By proceeding from difference to difference, and going to the point of ultimate difference, we finally gain access to inherent reality, which is that of completely specified being, individuated thanks to its differential 'form' which constitutes its essence, and governs its generic 'matter' (*Metaphysics*, 'Zeta', 12).

Or, if we diverge from a definitional thought of Being in order to think about the logic of processes, difference is still its logical element. Whether it is understood as difference from the other or from the self, it is the required departure point of all springing up and it is really what *promotes* the thing. For it is only by differentiating (oneself) that one becomes. Through it – in its *dia* – the dialectic opens up. This difference which is seen to be purely negative due to the rupture and the 'inequality'(*Ungleichheit*) it discloses is revealed to be the necessary condition for all self-development (thereby rising, in Hegelian terms, from the 'substance' to the 'subject' – see the 'Preface' to the *Phenomenology*, §3). When, in opposition to the prevailing standardization, the right to difference is invoked today, according to an influential saying of our age (or, as I would prefer to express it from my own perspective, the right to *divergence*, something I will justify later on), I believe one might also be drawing on this source, without perhaps taking sufficient notice of it. For we are not content with understanding this in the sense of an essentially conservative right to distinguish oneself from others and so elude normative levelling (which also goes for the rights of other cultures and all minorities). This would lead in other respects only to demands concerned purely with issues of identity. More than this, we propose the need for everyone, in a more essential way, to be able to have an intrinsic history which, through continual differentiation and surpassing, would make each of us equally possible *subjects*, as *cultural* subjects, containing within ourselves the possibility of self-promotion and an inventive future.

Yet, if we are well aware (albeit with a tacit knowledge) that standardization has assumed an increasing importance with globalization, we have perhaps not sufficiently measured the ways in which globalization suddenly hoists it up to a completely different level where it finds that a new definition has been conferred upon it. For globalization, taking standardization to its fullest and henceforth definitive extent, comprising as it does the whole of the globe, as I have said, due to this completion of closure, is precisely what has surreptitiously and without warning allowed the uniform to pass for a universal. By spreading this similarity everywhere, in other words on the scale of the whole planet, it definitively endorses it, without there being anything elsewhere (since there is no elsewhere) able even slightly to contradict it, except on a residual basis. This generality releases a false necessity because we are now a long way from just standardization of production in the realm of the economy and productivity. In the future what will count above all is that, by spreading not just extensively but really everywhere as a unique type, this will eradicate all other possibilities in advance. Properly speaking, these possibilities no longer have any place to exist; the uniform has imposed its standards as the only possible landscape, and it has done so without even seeming to have imposed them. This is how its discreet dictatorship is established.

We will inevitably find the same shop-window displays, the same hotels, the same keys, the same snapshots, the same posters of contentment and consumption in all four corners of the world. Finally closed in on itself, the (planetary) whole has ceased to do anything but reflect itself: a *self*-reflection which from now on constitutes the world under the reign of Similitude (and platitude) in a phantasmatic way. For if this is a dictatorship, it is one in which such standardization is not limited to material goods but overwhelms the imaginary. By means of successful editorial operations, *Harry Potter* or *The Da Vinci Code* (or any other product of the same type) formats the dreams of adolescents the world over in an identical way. Through its massive export of programmes, from one country to another, television effects its massacre. Otherwise anything, in some remote country, that still escapes this uniformity will be considered behind the times; or else, through tipping from the outdated into conservation, it will be placed in reserve, put in cellophane wrappers, and conscientiously protected in the great folklore of nations on the basis of an 'authentic' tradition. Worse still: the height of standardization is when an inevitably *kitsch* surface variation is added to the standard, so as to have us believe in the future promise of difference and discovery. At the top of buildings in Beijing, the roofs have been hiked up with eaves, which are underlined with glazed tiles and (why not?) prowling dragons to make it, *even so*, just a little Chinese. This is a way of adding a touch of exoticism and simulating the possibility of originality at negligible cost: to safeguard the myth of adventure and travel (by what ancestral memory does humanity still hold on to them?).

3 Yet I see thought strangely disarmed today in the face of the reign of uniformity which, by the fact that it has now reached the most distant parts of the planet, establishes its law – the law of occult force and not of right. And, beyond the feeling of loss, nostalgically experienced but with a feeling of self-induced guilt because it does not know how to accord with the new dimensions of things, this collective descent into the uniform is not really criticized: its *pseudo-universality* is not clearly analysed. Yet it is precisely in this, I believe, that the desire for dialogue between cultures encounters its principal obstacle as well as its greatest utility. For, if the surrounding standardization is considered to be the universal, whatever contains elements of the diversity of cultures (in a way that would not simply be conservationist or museological) is lost along with the plan (which might not be just imitation or assimilation) on which they could meet.

Therefore we are lacking this *plan*, in both senses of the word – as a project and as a work surface, isolated from the surrounding ideology, upon which we could operate; and as a type of perspective and representation from which a resistance to the standardization taking place could be envisaged. Perhaps it could even still be conceived analogically, if we were to go back to those old forms of art and knowledge like rhetoric and theodicy which today have been buried in the vaults. These appear to be outmoded discourses even though they were opportunely aware of how to inscribe difference into the heart of their concerns when faced with the risk of uniformity. Against this (*monoeideia*, as the Greeks had already expressed it), generating an overly equal tension which is therefore tiresome and 'monotonous' (*monotonia*), rhetoric recommended *varietas*, at once of tone, style and delivery (see Cicero, 2001: 106-8; Quintilian, 1920-2: XI, 3). Or, in this old argument which passed without a break from the Stoics to the Church Fathers and still found its place in classical philosophy whenever a need arose to justify God for his Creation (meaning that he had to be exculpated from the evil perceived everywhere as worming its way into it), delight was taken in demonstrating that God had to compose his world with difference, if he wanted it to be beautiful. He would have had to mingle shadows into the setting (in order to make the colours stand out), otherwise only a satiety would have been created through reproduction of the same, a sterile repetition to the point of saturation, a 'filling-up' (*sumplerôris*) and not a 'world' (*kosmos*). The failings, the imperfections, the tears, the violence and suffering, in short everything that is in general negative, necessarily – in other words 'logically' – introduced a 'multicoloured' (*poikilia*) salvation through intensity and attraction. Without it there would have been only lassitude. Paradise becomes difficult to describe as soon as, being homogenized as what is good, everything starts to look the same . . . The world is made more perfect, as Descartes (1996: IV) lucidly said, to the extent that I am myself imperfect.

III On the common

1 The common, a concept which is neither logical (and arising from reason) like the universal, nor economic (arising from production) like the uniform, but is political in its essence, lies at the other corner of the triangle: the common is what we are a part of or in which we take part, which is shared out and in which we participate. This is what makes it a 'political' concept in its origin: what is shared is what causes us to belong to the same city, that is to the *polis*. Aristotle's *Politics* begins with this notion of the common: 'We can see that any city is a sort of community' (*koinōnia*). A community is extensive as a principle, and this is so in these dimensions: in proportion at once to what is shared in it and to those who participate in it. It begins as two, that between man and woman, or master and slave, unfolding at the level of the house and then of the village, and finally of the city, to which all the other forms of community aspire and which, as far as Aristotle and all of the Greeks in the classical period were concerned, is its ultimate and perfect state.

As poor as the notion of the similar is, because, as we have seen, it is purely aspectual and relates to external features alone – being hardly any more substantial than a reflection – so that of the common serves as a strong concept, on which one can comfortably settle; it signals towards that never completely determinable ground, the groundless ground, from which, even without being able to measure it, we collectively draw, and whose resources we ceaselessly exploit. A community of life or work or anxiety or love or interest. We find in Georges Braque this laconic remark which already speaks volumes about the divergence, or rather the conflict, pitting against each other these two notions which we might at first sight be tempted to consider as equivalent (I especially like such reflections by painters who, wary of the excesses of theory, instantly know how to emphasize something: painting makes words seem suspect and goes straight to the facts): 'The common is true, the similar is false. Trouillebert resembles Corot, but they have nothing in common' (Braque, 1952). Trouillebert, say art dealers, is the poor-man's Corot. His foliage *resembles* that of Corot (blurred colours as at the beginning of autumn, slender birches or aspens beside empty paths and so on), but it *has nothing* of the atmosphere which constitutes the essence of the *Memories of Mortefontaine* or the landscapes of Morvan and that raises it to the level of Nervalian nostalgia. It is too speckled on the trunks which are themselves too heavily drawn – like telegraph poles. Another principle of Braque's could also, I believe, be taken for a motto – one which is valid not only for painters – as it goes straight to the point of rupture between them as if to a target: 'Look for the common which is not the similar' (Braque, 1952).

If, turning us towards the other side, facing the universal, we now measure the divergence in play in the same way, we see it becoming broader, no longer one of value (depth), but due to the perspective adopted. While the universal *decrees* (by way of 'you must' as a necessary law issued by reason) or, better, prior to any experience, *predicts*, the common, for its part, even if it doesn't acknowledge it or actually choose it, takes root, on the contrary, in experience; at once it is extended by it and enriches it (its most intense state is the commonality of lovers). I find myself already taken into the common (by my nature) and I also deliberately ground the common (in the City). What it contains as a precondition bears upon its originating or fundamental, but not necessary, character (its paradigm is the family), and this is also why it is a political concept: I decide to assume the relations of belonging I identify with or I invest in new ones (the political really being this place of concerted decision). It is even through the successive levels of the community of which I am (or am becoming) a part that I can define the various spheres of my existence. Similarly, while the universal bears its own extension from the outset to its completion in a categorical (and absolute) way, grasping the totality concerned as an imperative [*devoir-être*] which cannot accept any exceptions, the common, in contrast, is legitimate in its progression. Its extension is gradual: I am part of the common along with the people of my city – at another level, with my compatriots or, more fully, the state of the European community or the human community and 'family'; indeed, more broadly still, with all rational beings, including the gods (in Stoic cosmo-politism). Or, in a way that is regressive rather than progressive (stepping back from the political to the biological), I share the common with animals (the faculty of feeling) and more broadly with plants and everything in a living state (Aristotle's 'nutritive' soul), and so on. In this way, these various states of community gradually increase my existence, which is understood and extends by means of participation, from one end of the scale to the other, from genetic patrimony to the beloved person.

2 Nevertheless, isn't there a cut-off point at which the common will logically come to coincide with the universal – when the common is common to all (the members of the same class), and generic belonging is thereby universal for all of the elements concerned? One example is that all bodies have in common the fact that they are expanding, and this property is a universal attribute they have. This is verifiable even from the point of view of knowledge: isn't the apprehension of the common precisely what allows the concept to rise to the level of universality? Then rightly even those who, in the tradition of Aristotle, have wished to bring the two terms together have still (following Alexander of Aphrodisias and as has been analysed by Alain de Libera) needed to distinguish carefully between these two opposing levels: between the *abstraction* of the universal (as being of thought), on the one hand, and the *instantiation* of the common, as existence realised at the heart of these particulars, on the other (*instantiated*, as the English say – to be taken literally here in the sense of 'what is held inside'; 'subjected' or 'hypostasized' according to the textbook terms). In fact, buried as it is in scholasticism, this *distinguo* merits being drawn out of its oblivion so as to think about the relation between the two: on the one hand, the generic *universal*, engendered from individuals by abstraction and henceforth attaching itself to their nature from outside, remains for them a purely 'accidental' element; on the other hand, in contrast, this nature is in itself *common* as soon as it is realized in a 'material' which is that of the singular individual, even though only when within it. An essential difference of perspective therefore subsists even when the two categorical extensions completely match up: membership of the common is realized *in the thing* (*in re*), while the abstraction of the universal is 'ulterior' (*post rem*) to it. We will consequently be unable to associate the two notions without setting up a sluice gate between them to lessen the rupture between their levels of abstract or instantiated 'being'; or, without constructing a bridge between them linking territories which remain those of logical prescription on one side, and of evidence or decision on the other.

Yet, if we refer, for example, to the 'Universal' Declaration of Human Rights, which is presented at the same time, in its Preamble, as 'a common standard of achievement for all peoples and all nations', we see that the hiatus is not mediated but left entire between one and the other: between the abstraction of the universal *prescription*, on the one hand, and the commonality [*commun*] of *participation* on the other (or, to bring them closer to the modalities of being I have just evoked, between the level of *abstraction* of the first and the *instantiation* of the second). Hence the ambiguity that has been noted with regard to this subject. Or how, still in this preamble and without further articulation or only one in passing, could the 'universal respect' of rights and then, immediately after, the importance of their 'common understanding' be dealt with? (Why do these rights, if they are universal, require a *further* common understanding?) Even the association between the 'universal' and the 'effective', recurrent in the text and forming a notion, is not without its problems: does 'effective' here complete the predicate of universality established in principle (by radicalizing it) or rather compensate for it (by saving it from idealism)? We might think this question of logic is a matter of indifference for human destiny. I would think rather that, in not having known how to sort out these various relations, such a Declaration finally lapses into a formalism that, because it is not as rigorous, is even less convincing than the formalism associated with Kant that is so often mistrusted. Moreover, it will be noted that, in wanting to comment upon it and justify it without passing through these necessary *distinguos*, many of these formulations today come up against the drawback of concession, which they illogically add to the enactment of universality: 'almost no one', we are told, dares openly to challenge these human rights; they enjoy a 'quasi universal' recognition, and so on (see, for example, Hersch, 1999).

For the universal neither tolerates such approximations nor accepts being even slightly eroded in this way. It either exists or it does not, since it would be unable to renounce its absolute status (as law). But, on the other hand, nothing would be more unwelcome than to consider the common to be a low-grade or less demanding universality, or to make it play the role of a crutch for the universal to use, under the pretext that it is anchored and certified in existence (that it is, according to the required terms, not 'in thought' but 'instantiated'). For the common also has its ideality, its characteristic and fully fledged ideality – precisely that, deriving from experience, of being able to increase in extent as in intensity. Likewise, when we see the emphasis today swerving from one pole to the other, from the universal to the common (as, for example, Madame Delmas-Marty's (2007) plea for a common 'law' testifies), it is in fact, under cover of explanation, a question of a significant slippage that demands analysis: beneath the discreetly operated reorientation it is actually the whole horizon that is altered.

This reorientation does not mean, as is often too simplisticly believed, that we have become more realistic (or less utopian), but really that the perspective should be displaced from morality to politics or, to use the earlier terms, from that of the *prescription* (enactment) to that of *participation*; that the imperative [*devoir-être*] is consequently considered less as established beforehand than as needing to be taught and conquered. Thus, when one doggedly maintains as a decisive, indeed conclusive, fact that, of the 180 States which reaffirmed the Universal Declaration at the World Conference on Human Rights in Vienna in 1993, not even a third of them had signed it in 1948 (Delmas-Marty, 2007: 202), I believe this translates as indicating that the common has since that time overridden the universal within our range of concern (or that the point of view of progressive extension has overridden that of the principle of aggregation, or that adhesion has overridden enactment, and so on). Or perhaps its baton has simply been passed on: with the universal on the point of faltering, the common is what would legitimately replace it.

3 Moreover, we will perhaps be missing an element of what the common and its possibilities mean if we are just satisfied with the Greek term (*koinos*). The Latin is *com-munis* and so it enriches the common by giving it another dimension: it does not simply designate what is shared and is operated together through its prefix (*cum*: 'with'), but may also be understood, as the root of the word implies, as what arises from both the gift and the obligation (*munus*). This offers another angle from which to explore how full-fledged ideality is created from the *com-mon*. Roberto Esposito (2009) very appropriately reminds us that the *munus* is a gift, but it is one marked by its character of reciprocity that remains implicit (according to its root in Indo-European languages denoting

exchange). What therefore prevailed in *munus* was the reversibility of the gift. The Latin term would thereby more directly point towards this enigmatic ground I evoked at the start, the groundless ground, which all community was perceived to draw upon from the moment the idea of it being a supplementary property – or the simple product – of the subjects it assembles (both remaining external to them) was abandoned. It is *com-munis*, literally the one who shares a responsibility (for a task or a function) with others – indeed, who is considered to fulfil an office (the *immunis* is dispensed with).

These considerations are important if we want to think about the political nature of the common and remove the ambiguity it contains. For if the common is what I share with others, it is also, due to this fact and following this dividing line (which also stands as a line of demarcation), that which excludes all others. Or, if the opposite of the common is neither the individual or the singular (which are opposed to the universal), nor the different (which is opposed to the uniform), but rather the *inherent* or the *particular*, we also see that this adverse 'inherent' none the less threatens to absorb it and, consequently, totally to overturn its ideal. This takes place as soon as this community of sharing considers that it possesses its shared attributes *in its own right*: as soon as what opened its members up to one another then closes up in a common property. Designating an inside, it ejects outside. Therefore the common is a term with a Janus face: it is at once inclusive and exclusive. It can just as well open as close, oppose the inherent and identify with it. A defensive reversal corresponds to its expansive space. In effect it calls on the one hand for participation and is extensive; it ensures 'communication' through differences and it continually unites within a single system. Such is the *open* common, for example, of 'common sense'. But, on the other hand, this common can equally well, by closing its frontiers, sharpen its borders into cutting edges and its outskirts into fortifications. It then casts out into the void (that is, outside of its plenitude) those who do not participate in it; literally, it *ex-communicates*. Such is the characteristic that is the flip-side of all 'communitarisms'. We continually see this in the political – or rather (because they are opposed to sharing), anti-political – demonstrations in contemporary societies.

To grasp the common by its roots (from *munus*, from accountability, from gift – duty, from obligation) fortunately obstructs this ambivalence. By thereby implying what is void or defective in the relationship of exchange which links us to others, at the same time we conjure up the temptation to make this sharing of the community an exclusive and positive privilege, rejecting its defects by casting them out. If the community conceives of itself under the sign of *munus*, of debt and gift, the relation of belonging upon which the communitarian feeling would readily rely, and which forms its comfort, sees itself in a salutary way turned back to dependency. A whole current of contemporary thought is committed to this breach (no doubt inspired by Marcel Mauss and making its echoes felt at the edges of phenomenology – Derrida, Nancy, Marion, Esposito and so on). Wanting to found the community otherwise than according to the logical categories which would be directly carried over onto the political, judging them from that moment not fit for purpose, it has precisely argued for this originating reciprocity of debt and gift in order to dismantle the image of *full* subjects, of which the community would simply be the excrescence. Once such subjects adopt the communitarian attributes as a property, they are then seen as expropriating them for themselves: from the *munus*, which grounds their relation, the community is literally what *dis-obliges* them. They would therefore no longer draw upon any principle of identification within it. And because of this the path of identitarian closure, which is always the threat facing the communitarian, is barred. From that point on philosophy has amply justified it: the vocation of the community should not be to enclose, but to dis-enclose. Indeed, the history of the common, at the heart of the political transformation of ancient Greece, had already set off in this direction.

IV From the advent of the State to the cosmo-political extension of the common

1 The fact that the common is 'political' in nature can be shown in the advent of the City, the *polis*. Through it the idea of the common was born and gradually assumed definition, and did so from the most ancient times. The common is the essence of the Greek city and at the same time the city identifies itself with the idea of the common. Its genealogy can be traced back beyond this to Homer's narratives. Marcel Detienne (1999: ch. 5) has shown how this commonality was inscribed in space during the assembly of warriors, when it assumed the form of 'setting in the middle', at an equal distance from the participants, so putting in place a reciprocal and reversible relation between the warriors that would be beyond distinctions of rank. Whether at the time the booty was shared or at the prize giving during funeral games,[1] carrying 'to the centre' (*es meson*) rather than passing from hand to hand had already assumed a pre-institutional character which de-privatized relations and de-personalized positions. In the same way, anyone who wanted to address the assembly always had to do so from the centre, signifying that what he had to say was of concern to all. Thus the transition from warriors, whom we imagine sitting in a circle in order to share women, weapons and booty, to the formation of the agora[2] in the centre of the city, inaugurating a public space and founding the word on a relation of equality (the *isegoria*), is apparent and undermines the idea of there being some great historical rupture (a Greek 'miracle') from which classical reason would have been born. For, in gradually being separated from the ambiguous statements of the exceptional being with fabulous powers, the one who is divine, the magus, the poet or the Master of truth, pronouncing his judgements, a new word, from magic to logic, became the prerogative of all by being shared. Expounded 'in the middle', it pleads equally for and against, appeals for approval, establishes its reasons and opens up the discussion, so separating the collective from the private. In so doing, it detaches the primacy of the common from any particular interests.

I don't see any more convenient entry point into the idea of the common, born as it was from that of sharing, than by following how it thereby developed from and in history, since history is effectively its driving force. From the group of warriors to the people of the city, from the *laos* to the *demos*, we already see the common extending and shaping the embryonic jurisdictions in pre-classical Greece at the same time as the conduct of war was being transformed (and that, breaking with single and hand-to-hand combats, from the time of Homer, the phalange was being developed as an instrument of military democratization). In parallel, the idea not only of a *common place* but of a *common good* (*xunon*, *agathon*) transcending particular interests, starts to take shape. The diametrical antithesis of these two (the 'common' / the 'particular') is put in place and a value judgement is grafted onto it – indeed, all supreme value flows from it. By raising itself to the measure of all, the *common* begins to raise the idea of sharing to the level of an absolute principle.

Decrees of experience like these cannot satisfy us: 'expenses seem easier to accept when they are shared' (Democritus, fr. 279), or, inversely, 'poverty experienced in common is more difficult to accept' ('than the poverty suffered by individuals, because there is no hope of mutual help') (Democritus, fr. 287). It is still useful to cite this passage from Democritus in its entirety because it explicitly founds the ideal of the Greek City on the common: 'The highest importance has to be given to affairs of State so that it may be well governed and one should refuse to involve oneself in quarrels contrary to equity, or succumb to the temptation to acquire a power contrary to the common interest. The well-run State is the greatest protection, and contains within it all things; when this is safe, all is safe; when it is destroyed, all is destroyed' (fr. 252). Since it is at the level of the common alone (*to tôu xunôu*), founding the City, that the fate of individuals is decided, in the eyes of the Greeks, and as though they had no hesitation about the nature of the political, good political governance will logically be embodied in the supremacy of the common over the interests of the individual. The theories of Plato and Aristotle thereafter did no more than develop this conception. Whether they instigate the power of a single one, a small number, or the majority, good constitutions have no other criterion except to be concerned with the common interest, while deviant constitutions are only interested in the profit of particular interests (Aristotle, *Politics*: III, 7).

2 In fact, philosophy's task, as it assumed the destiny of the common at the heart of the Greek City, was to accomplish two things at once (here philosophy has really already taken up its role of thought-which-arrives-late-at-the-party). On the one hand, it extended the demand this involved by envisaging a broader community than that of the group, the clan, the territory and even the City, and consequently deploying the idea of a sharing that goes beyond even politics. But at what other level could this be established? On the other hand and in parallel, it has to establish the value of the reign and status of the common triumphing over the particular. Such is the double movement which we see magnificently fulfilled in Heraclitus. In his work the common exceeds the limitations of belonging and becomes common to all through the founding of a community of the mind. Let's not accept these banal thoughts, but read in them the strength of their emergence and the immensity of what they open up. 'Thinking is common to all' (Heraclitus, *Fragments*, Diels-Kranz: 113; or 'to know themselves and think effectively is shared by all people', fr. 116). For human beings the common has intelligence as its foundation, as Heraclitus had said. This common is above all conceived in a meticulous way to be the point or geometrical middle at which oppositions are abolished (thus: 'Beginning and end have a common place within the circumference of a circle', fr. 103). It is the place at which the one opens completely to the other, where frontiers dissolve in the face of unity, where antagonisms are broken down, where partialities are mopped up; it is where contradiction is suspended. This common of de-exclusion is in fact nothing but the divine itself (according to the supreme expression which associates without the slightest mediation of contraries: 'God is day-night, war-peace, winter-summer, satiety-hunger', fr. 67).

This other expression is radiant through its confidence in what, as 'discourse', then has the potential of becoming reason, *logos*: 'The *logos* is common to all, even though in living most people treat thought as though it belonged to them alone' (fr. 2). They believe they can communicate with one another by repeating words they have learned, which are continually being handed on, but each of them nonetheless remains blissfully ignorant of this appeal by the word (of the demands it makes). They remain separate in the flux of their own vague thought and make no effort to sound out the commonality [*commun*] that these words involve (as it maintains the passivity and somnolence of the mind by means of an illusion of a continuous sharing and extending everywhere, doesn't the modern myth of Communication still largely rest on this snare?). Henceforth, do these 'most people' actually 'live'? Rather, they are still 'sleeping'. Heraclitus says this with so much greater force because his epoch did not allow the concrete and symbolic to become completely separated from one another: it is necessary to *wake up*, he tells us, in order to raise oneself up to the common. Thus, 'For those who are awake there is one common world, but all of those who are asleep have withdrawn into a private world of their own' (fr. 89). During the night, it is easy to see, each person withdraws into a separate world, his world, that of his singular phantasms and codes: nocturnal worlds are compartmentalized, they are not shared. To fall asleep, in other words, is to abandon the transparency of the common. It is to withdraw into the opaque thickness of one's own life, to enclose oneself in one's own silent regulations to the point of becoming absorbed in them, cutting the bridges and effecting a secession in thought. To sleep is to sink into one's 'natural simplicity'. Then, in the face of this night-enfolding, this night plunging again into the heart of the private as into the Erebus,[3] the common is *access*, above all to the common of the shared word; this is why it requires 'awakening' (see also: 'We should not act or speak like those who are asleep', fr. 73).

In other words it is only by and in the unity of the common that *the* world (the only world, the actual one, disengaged from the amorphousness of vague thought) is conceived and constructed. Hence this formula definitively anchors the political in philosophy: either that of the common of the City in the common perceived by the mind, or else what becomes the law of men in the Law of things. For both are grasped in the same vital process, a pure level of speculation that, in Heraclitus, had not yet been detached to the point that would allow two disconnected blocs to take shape, so forming the two tomes of philosophy that are knowledge and action. This still leaves us in the state of unitary thought, condensed as it emerges, confident in its source, discovering its power and not yet having any doubt about it, in which effectivity is complete and doesn't allow itself to be dispersed into various and rival sections. It is only by building upon the common, as Heraclitus tells us, by exploiting its possibilities, that we can through the same action do both things at once: to *com-prehend* the world (in other words to grasp it in its correlations which make it come about), and bring people together in *co-habitation*. Finally we can draw 'strength' only from the common, whether it is a matter of thinking or governing; both consist only in its activation. Thus: 'those who speak with intelligence necessarily draw their strength from what is common to all, as the city does from the law, but they do so even more strongly' (fr. 114).

3 Even so, a lot of time will have had to pass (all the slowness and violence of History) before such an access to what impresses itself upon the vigilance of the mind as the necessity for a *common world* (*koinos kosmos*) could find expression in social and political terms. If the common was developed from and under the impulse of History, there was also an immense amount of resistance to it over its course. In other words, if human laws go back to the same 'intelligence' of the common as their unique source, in the way Heraclitus affirms, they would be unable to escape from the circumscriptions which enclose them as casually as the law of things perceived by reason. The form of exclusion the common bears on its flip-side is obviously withdrawn with a lot more difficulty when we go back down from the order of *logos* to that of the City. It is even precisely this break which stretches out History, as it appears retrospectively to us today, and underlies its advance (otherwise an indelibly messianic meaning may be found it it). The common of the *logos* emerging from the political common serves in contrast, in so far as it is a regulatory idea, as an ideal or a horizon to the political common entangled in social affairs. And aren't we currently at that precise moment when such a break begins to allow us only a glimpse of its possible absorption? Such at least would be the positive side of globalization when faced with the risk of uniformity.

In fact aren't we aware that the Greek City cast out just as much as (or even more than) it brought together while it was still in the Classical age? It united its citizens by giving them a share of civil rights and duties, which it refused to all others (women, foreigners, outsiders, slaves). Thales bears witness to this. Ordinarily he is remembered as the first person to have openly oriented Greek thought towards rational knowledge by thinking of all things according to a single and common principle: water. This would make him the first to have awakened to an understanding of the common. But we also note that he was responsible for this highly segregationist saying (others even attribute it to Socrates): 'He loved to say that he thanked his good fortune for three things: to be a human and not an animal, to be a man and not a woman and finally to be a Greek and not a barbarian' (in Diogenes Laertius, 1853: VII).

Plato is divided in this respect. Certainly (working in the opposite way), he was the first to approach a conception of the 'human genus', but we also see that the function of exclusion from the common, far from being abstracted, is redoubled in his City. Such is really the ambiguity of the common: the more intensified it is, the more exclusive it becomes (love testifies to this). Thus it is not only within the restricted frame of the City, but again within the limits of a particular class (of 'guardians'), ostensibly cutting themselves off from others and carefully purifying themselves in relation to them, that Plato undertook to fence off the common through political measures. Within such a narrow perimeter, it could then be extended to all things and to everyone (*Republic*, V). This absolutization of the common enters into the service of what becomes the State: holding everything in common (no longer having anything personally owned) is the unique condition by which it is saved from the corruption with which it is intrinsically threatened by a retreat into the particular. In giving way like this to the fascination of the common, indeed trying for the first time – at least in a systematic way – to eliminate ownership in the form of the private, Socrates (in Plato) proposes to extend common possession not only to all goods but also to women and children, and even to feelings, thus outlining at a stroke the horizon of any form of 'communism'. The only boundary this placing in common encountered was the body. Socrates anticipated this limit. We can share everything: houses, women, children and even feelings, commune in joy and pain, but the body remains inexorably of the order of the personal and the particular. What arises from the body, Socrates concludes, is not shared: the body is the insurmountable enclosure of the private (or a level other than politics will have to be set up, one which would be mystical – hence the 'communion' at which the Body of Christ is to be shared).

The Greeks in contrast were a lot more timid in envisaging going beyond the framework of their City especially regarding whether they should extend commonality [*commun*] to 'others', to those who were not fellow-citizens or who were strangers. In classical Greece, where the frontier between Greek and Barbarian was still far from being lowered, it was only 'between us', between Greeks – because they were of the same origin – that it was possible to speak, not really of war, but only of 'discord' (*stasis*, *The Republic*, 470 b–c). Going beyond ethnic group-ings, beyond the isolated worlds of the cities, is still only seen in a distant utopia: until we have philosophers who become kings, or kings with the wisdom of philosophers, 'dear Glaucon, there will be no release from the evils suffered by cities, nor even, I think, from those of the human genus' (*Republic*, 473 d). Therefore as modestly as the notion of a 'human genus' makes its entrance here (by no more than amplification in a passage at the end of the sentence) the condition placed in relation to it, and from the outset acknowledged to be ridiculous, has none the less had an effect, for it is only in the light of this new power of the philosopher-king, which has not yet occurred and is even considered fanciful – as power therefore illuminated by *logos* (that is a politics finally become rational) – that the idea of a community of all people can be given a shape. What undoubt-edly deserves to be generalized, and is applicable to what comes later, is that the political extension of the common, the rejection of its exclusive character, goes hand in hand with the affirmation of rationalism; or, putting it in a different way, that particularism, communitarianism and segregation have always been advocated by drawing upon the sources of an anti-rationalism.

4 The step was taken slowly, and this crossing over, into a world where the frontiers were about to fall, is instructive for us at a time of globaliza-tion. For the Greeks had to wait for the collapse of the internal order of the City (perched on its founding narratives, its myth of indigenousness, its gods and laws), before the idea of the common might extend farther, carried along by Stoicism. In Greece the cities lost their autonomy after Alexander's conquests and greater empires prevailed. In Cyprus, for example, where the Stoic Chrysippe was born at the beginning of the third century BCE, power, under the influence of great rival realms, was continually passing from one dominant authority to another, from Macedonians to Syrians or Egyptians. Under this continual change

of masters, attachment to a single homeland becomes impossible; any political exclusivity unravels. Similarly, while justice and the law were considered before Stoicism as inseparable from certain social and political forms – the City, the *polis*, which took the place of both State and society – thereafter they were judged as suitable to govern the relations between all people, at the same level of moral equality. In consequence they became independent of their particular provenance and of the framework of the City.

> Even before the emergence of Stoicism, Diogenes the Cynic, when asked where he came from, replied: 'I am a citizen of the world', *kosmopolites eimi*. The reference to any origin or precise place was thereby placed between parentheses, and citizenship was promoted to the level of the whole world. Did Diogenes mean that he could be at home anywhere in the whole universe? Any other assignment would be too narrow and would erroneously constrain his humanity. Nevertheless this expression is not at all to be understood as referring to anything resembling a political entity, like an empire such as Alexander's, being extended to its furthest limits, but here the idea of the 'world', *kosmos*, assumes an essentially moral significance and means that the whole of the world is ordered, that a unique and divine principle, which is properly rational, *logos*, passes through it from one end to the other, extending not only to all people, but equally to the race of the gods and together forming the 'great family' of reasonable beings. Once we have seen this norm alone assimilating nature to reason, and in accordance with which all people must lead their lives, any lesser degree is erased, and any intermediary dependency is abolished. The common of the world is the common of reason shared. 'The nature of man is such that there exists a natural law between man and the human genus . . . in the world or the city commune', *in urbe mundove communi*, we read in Cicero as he sums up such an ideal (*De finibus*: III, 20, 67); or again, we read in Stobæi (1860: 40, 9) that the world, *kosmos*, is the 'common land of all people', *koine patris*.[4]
>
> To be fully entitled to belong to this common world, conceived on the 'cosmic' scale, within which specific cities are henceforth said to be nothing but houses, it is enough 'to be a man',

whether one was born Greek or barbarian, whether descended from a royal lineage or a servile condition. In this, Stoicism, in the name of the common, goes beyond all immediate categorizations and localizations, equalizes ranks and conditions, and makes an abstraction of epochs. The transformation is significant in relation to the earlier time when people originated in a race, a clan or a territory. 'The world is the only relation common to all', whether these people would be considered 'as liberated, slaves or people who come from elsewhere' (Seneca, 2011; III, 28). Nothing human, in fact, according to an expression that has become famous and turned into a motto, can be regarded as 'foreign' to us; all people find themselves as fellow-citizens of the world, linked together by a community of fate which is to bring to perfection their only really justified belonging, that which links them to nature (see Cicero: the only 'society' founded in reason is that of the 'human genus' which is, above everything else, 'in conformity with nature' (Cicero, 1913: V, 21)). Likewise, when he goes back to his city, as specific as it is, the Stoic judges it in the name of this order of the world considered as a whole, according to the law of Zeus, on a global scale. He can without difficulty relativize its constitution and laws and consider their particularity as arbitrary and conventional; at the very least suspending this citizenship of birth in the light of his world citizenship.

The fact remains that, as we can without difficulty deduce from their system even though their texts are lost today, the Stoics did not conceive of any constitution of a cosmopolitan type beyond these basic positions, outlining a legal framework for such a world citizenship along the lines of the constitutions from which Plato and Aristotle established the plan for the City. For them, this improvement upon established political frame-works still had an essentially moral nature and they did not manage to find an institutional and political translation. Even if, for a Stoic thinker at the end of Antiquity – and one, moreover, who was an Emperor (Marcus Aurelius: IV, 4) – all people are supposed to constitute part of the same civic body, and 'the world itself is therefore really like a city', this authority of the law does not for all that come from the State, but from reason alone, and this thought of a common political organ, *politeuma*, ultimately remains abstract. Cosmopolitanism has developed its ideal of wisdom over so many centuries without touching upon the sovereignty of States. This has been to such an extent that political institutions able to transgress particular sovereignties and be common to the entire world have only recently been established, at the conclusion of actual 'world' wars, and this remains an astonishingly new task for our age.

At least this would be the optimistic version of contemporary history. For we could wonder whether the opposite is not, in fact, operating underneath it; if this cosmopolitan humanism which, through its utopia, which has until now ceaselessly worked upon European consciousness, in continuing ancient Stoicism, is not in the end actually in the process of dying before our very eyes. Doesn't globalization, which has today finally globalized humanity in relation to itself and effectively unified it, operate under the pressure of factors that are completely different from moral and cultural values based upon emancipatory virtue? Hence the fact that at one and the same time it completely eludes the universalist aspiration, rendering it obsolete.[5]

V The other level: the universal as a logical category of philosophy

1 Faced with this political extension of the common, stretching as it did over centuries and closely linked with the emergence and then the decline of the City, it appears clear that the universal has a different provenance – and is different in substance. It proceeds from another source one which, among the Greeks, is internal to *discourse*, that is *logos*, as founder of 'logic'. While the common takes a long time to come to the surface, emerging through the unfolding and violence of History, the universal is understood from the outset to be on the operative level of knowledge. Its birth came like a flash in the history of thought. Like Athena from the head of Zeus, it burst forth equipped with the arms of philosophy. Heraclitus, musing about the *logos*, had already put it on its way as if sending it into orbit: 'the wise are those who listen not to me but to the discourse' ('to agree that all is one'), he said, in the most laconic way. *Not to me*, but to the *discourse* . . . That you should not be listening to me when I speak (as a philosopher), but to the discourse itself, expresses the starting point of philosophy. In fact what is being played out in this powerfully proclaimed dissociation is a major event: thought ostensibly cuts its ties with the *individuality* of a subject. To make a claim to truth, the discourse-reason detaches itself in an autonomous instant by displaying its separation from the 'self' which expresses it. It must be of equal value for all and it is therefore placed equidistant from each person, including its author. It is totally indifferent, and even becomes ice-cold, in relation to its own origin. Ascetically disengaged from its intimate rootedness, to philosophize (haven't we forgotten this today?) does not mean to describe something.

In order for the hypothesis to be properly assessed, it is time (even if only for a moment) to get out of the habit of this condition of the possibility of truth to which, as for Orpheus, there is no possibility of ever returning, but that we have assimilated so well thanks to the proven success of science. In order for the hypothetical to weigh equally over thought, by being considered in relation to other cultures which have been unaware of it, then it has to be examined in its emergence, whose demand from that moment on has ceased to have any 'necessity' about it (against the renowned 'necessary development' of the human mind). In raising the *logos* to the level of an autonomous power, this act of secession possesses a rigour that is also strange and consequently inventive. The *logos*, in order to be probing, must make an object of a *homo-logia*, to use the Greek words of Heraclitus as he made its vocation explicit. It is required literally to be 'homo-logued': the *logos* demands not only to be always recognized as the 'same' (*homos*), unvarying, but also that everyone must agree to consider it in the 'same' way. At one and the same time, it would be 'always' (fr. 1, 'of this discourse which always exists', *aei ón*, at least if one cuts the sentence in this way) and no exceptions can be accepted. Even if he does not yet define it as such, 'all is one' is a universal truth as far as Heraclitus is concerned. Consequently he instigated a model of exposition for philosophy, from discourse which at first rushed presumptuously to grasp the 'whole', and then became (Heraclitus here opens up a path) the one which grasps 'according to the whole'. In other words, in a universal way, which also means conceptually (*kat-holou*).

It will not be possible to clarify why the universal has acquired such a hegemonic status in European thought, despite the risk of arousing, in fits and starts, the revolt of the individual demanding to be unique (as substance – as subject – as other) as a backlash, unless we start by understanding how this promotion of the universal, as a demand from reason, goes together with its elevation to the concept, as a tool of philosophy. Or rather the one does not accompany the other, but it is a question of the same operation (from which philosophy is, as if 'by a miracle', so nimbly born): the status of the universal is included in the very production of the concept. It is at once its condition and consequence: the universal gives its 'logical' form (of *logos*) to the concept, which stabilizes the universal and renders it operative for knowledge. They understand each other in the same abstraction. Likewise, by way of consequence, coming at it from the other direction, if other cultures have not posed the problem of the universal, it is precisely because they have not, as the Greeks did, erected – separated – a level of the concept, the only place at which true knowledge is acquired.

2 For having done this, 'Socrates' plays a major role (which really definitively makes him the Father of philosophy). As Aristotle tells us

in his reflections on ethics, he was the first to 'seek' 'according to the whole' and, at the same time, to 'fix thought on definitions' (*Metaphysics*, A, 6; M, 4). 'According to the whole' (*kat-holou*) would be the Greek way of expressing the universal. As for 'definitions', they are effectively what Socrates aimed at by starting with the diversity of examples and phenomena (thus various examples of courage, or manifestations of beauty, would reveal what Courage or Beauty are in themselves or in their essence, i.e. according to their definition and covering every possible meaning), using induction (*epagógé*) to move the mind towards the unity of the concept. So the contribution of Socrates, according to the first historian of philosophy (which is what Aristotle was), really relates to this operative mutation concerning the problem of the whole (*holon*). Unlike the *phusiologoi*, whom we call the 'pre-Socratics' precisely due to this rupture, Socrates was not preoccupied with the 'whole' of nature but, by seeking 'according to the whole' (*kat-holou*), he made the 'whole' into a formal (or logical) exigency. After this to philosophize would no longer mean enquiring *about* the whole of the world, taken as an object, nor even about the principle of this whole, but rather thinking 'in conformity with the whole', in the mode of the whole: in other words, in the mode of universality – that is, thinking conceptually.

The originality we ordinarily attribute to Socrates, touching upon the shift in thought he brought about, from one domain to the next, which is in fact the most visible one (to have passed from physical to moral questions), is therefore to be understood in this sense. Did the mind experience its first disenchantment here? No longer having the juvenile urgency (or the naive hope or salutary illusion) of directly and all at once laying his hands on the entirety of things, as the first thinkers did with so much audacity, Socrates then transformed the 'whole'. Instead of being a certain 'thing' (water, air, infinitude, and so on), it became a *rule*. No longer able to instantiate it in things, he turned it back onto discourse. He turned it into an internal condition, as a rule which fixes both its (universal) validity and constitutes its (conceptual) operativity. In so doing, learning to think 'according to the whole', or universally, Socrates makes us forget the dream of being able to express total truth in a word and so sets (forces) thought onto the hard road of its rigour.

The Greeks drew from this a major conception which will not be brought into question again: the elevation of thought is confused with access to universality. This even constitutes the first action of philosophy (which Aristotle therefore describes at the beginning of his *Metaphysics*, A, 1): at the start (at the lower level) is sensation which is always individual (of the reign of the *hekaston*), raised up from the here and now. Aristotle leaves it in passing as self-evident, but through it he launches European thought onto a path from which there will be no turning back: 'We do not ordinarily consider any of our sensations (*aesthesis*) to be wisdom' (or 'science': *sophia*). *Sophia*, in other words, is in leaving the singular of sensation, and knowing will be definitively separated from the flavour of things. *Flavour* and *knowing*[1] are effectively opposed, as are the individual and the universal, because flavour is precisely the inexhaustible enjoyment of the individual, as the contrary of knowledge directed towards the universal: 'flavoursomeness' penetrates into this individual so as to let infinitely fleeting oneness emanate from him, while knowing is constructed ascetically on its renunciation. This is why, sensing its most stubborn irreducible other, Aristotle is careful not to raise it into a rival notion, which would open up another path, but hastily turns away from it.

What then does Aristotle regard as constituting 'experience'? Not the absorption by the present singularity of lived sensation in an inexhaustible way, but rather the piling-up of these multiple sensations which are deposited in the memory, due to their cross-referencing: this is already an *identity* that has issued from the diverse. The mastery of 'art' and 'knowledge' will itself finally be attained only when, by the enthronement of this logic, 'a single universal judgement, applicable to all in similar cases, is freed from a multitude of experimental notions' (the *hupolepsis* is the judgement that possesses this character of universality). In fact, 'when Callias was sick, forming a judgement about whether a particular remedy helped him to recover, and whether the same thing happened in the case of Socrates and in many other individual cases, was a matter of experience'; but to judge that such a remedy would relieve 'all individuals of such a constitution, within the limits of a determined class, when they were affected by such a sickness', moves us, by the fact that it is in principle a matter of an entire class, on to the universality of a knowledge which is no longer empirical, but has become 'theoretical'.

It is true that Aristotle was quite willing to recognize that this empirical knowledge can, from a practical point of view, prevail over knowing that would only be notional and arise from the *logos*, effectively for the reason that the first is a knowledge of the individual and the second of the universal (then, in fact, Aristotle reasonably states, we always treat an *individual*: someone in particular, Callias or Socrates, and not man in general). All the same, as to the quality of knowing considered – that of the universal – allowing it to emerge from the simple statement in order to establish the cause from it, will mean that it will always prevail over the other. Wouldn't there be a contradiction here? No, at least not from the time that, through this primacy accorded to universality, Greece effectively opted for the abstract and the speculative, detached from practice and valorized above it (even in the work of the pragmatic Aristotle). The expression is in conclusion: 'The knowledge of all things necessarily belongs to the one possessing the science of the universal to the highest degree, because he knows about every case in a certain way' (Aristotle, *Metaphysics*, part 2).

3 Two consequences result from this, pulling in opposite directions and from that point on establishing the problematic condition of universality for European thought. On the one hand, universality is inherent to science, and goes hand in hand with the necessary character of its pronouncements. Science, as Aristotle notes, is not in fact distinguished from opinion by the true or false character of its affirmations (since there are also true opinions and the object of one and the other may be the same), but by the character of necessity which attaches to the propositions that are stated by the former: opinion envisages in terms of the contingent (as that which can be other than what it is) what science envisages precisely as not being able to exist any other way. For it is only from what cannot be otherwise that there can be definition and demonstration (and if science were to treat the contingent, it would immediately make it necessary). Hence it follows that the first and founding knowing is that of *axioms*, since these embrace the universality of beings *a priori*, and not some particular genre to the exclusion of others. In stating a universal and necessary truth, axioms do not simply belong to all particular beings, without any exceptions, but go back as far as the link Being [*Être*] maintains with

itself, as Being [*Être*] 'as being [*être*]', in the absolute sense (such is the exemplary universality of the principle of non-contradiction, prior to all of them, because it is 'unconditioned', and which is only the negative formulation of the principle of identity at the foundation of Being – see Aristotle, *Metaphysics*, 'Gamma', 3). This absolute universality of axioms is definitively linked to the fact that they are only an analysis of the idea of 'being' [*être*]. The universality of logic therefore leads us back, at the heart of Greek thought, to the level of the ontological. Hence the question one can no longer *logically* fail to ask is this: what will happen to its necessary exigency in thinking which has not, like that of the Greeks, thought according to the *fold* of Being (since they would therefore not have conceived of knowing from axioms either)?

Therefore Greek thought had already established the *prescriptive* character of the universal, beyond a basic generality of acknowledgement, founding the imperative [*devoir-être*] of definition and science and which we saw Kant transpose, as such, from knowledge to the laws of morality. And so the question posed at the outset is revived in a compelling way and made precise, having assumed a cultural depth in the meantime. Don't we still see this axiomatic character if not inhabiting at least haunting the ideality of principles that we today present as universal? The question, via Aristotle, can even now be considered from one step further on – indeed, it leads us right to the edge of the cliff, facing the sheer drop. It becomes disturbing to the extent that we can never get away from it. For we also need properly to take into account the other consequence pulling in the opposite direction and which, ever since Aristotle, we see being affirmed in a parallel way. At the same time as it is the science, or *logos*, only of the universal – the *logos* becoming the discourse of science – it is, on the other hand, only the individual, that is, a particular person or tree, as I see them, that one or 'this one' (*todi*, see *Metaphysics*, 'Zeta', 12-15), which *actually exists*. I treat this individual who is here and not man in general. Such is the dilemma (and the trauma) which we can see take hold of European thought from the time that, along with Aristotle, it too conveniently abandoned establishing a level of Ideas separated from the realm of the senses and opinion, on which to perch the universal and into which true Being would be able to withdraw (see Jullien, 2006: ch. 11).

'Existence is comprised of individuals, while science is concerned with universals' (*Existentia est singularium, scientia est de universalibus*): this has been presented since medieval times as an adage, acknowledging the contradiction. On the one side, there is that which composes existence itself, or what makes it an intimate reality, by way of various singularities; on the other side, there is the only thing 'about this' that concerns science, and then at a distance (*de*: the relation is external). What breach, impossible to fill in, was thereby created between the two? For, on the one hand, from that point on it was proved that 'it is only from the universal and from form that there is definition' (*Metaphysics*, 'Zeta', 11), and therefore that there is science. But at the same time only the individual is real, only he is the essence (at least as primary essence) – that is, Socrates or Callias, this man here. On the other hand, 'man in general, the horse in general, and other terms of this sort, which are affirmed from a multiplicity of individuals, by way of the universal predicate, are not a substance' (rather, Aristotle puts it in technical terms, 'a composite determined by a certain form, and of a certain matter itself considered universally' ('Zeta', 10). 'Man' as a concept, considered in terms of the universal, is only a generic attribute, conferred from the outside (in an abstract way) and existing only in an 'accidental' way when it comes to this man. The question thus posed effectively opens an abyss in European thought and to a certain extent has formed its fate. In its application it becomes for us this question: when we deal with something like 'human rights' are we still, by declaring them universal, depending on this abstract universality?

VI First encounter of the universal and the common: Roman citizenship extended to the Empire

1 When confronted with the Greek heritage, what did Rome bring not only to it but also to the divisions it raised and the exclusions it left? Ordinarily Rome is credited precisely with having taken further, into the heart of the 'concrete', that of History and its institutions, the exigency of universality that philosophy has defined. But how exactly should this be understood if we do not want to content ourselves overly complacently with setting in motion those great simplistic binaries which, seen from afar, make the history of civilization seem like interconnections foreseen ahead of time (Greeks/Romans, abstract/concrete, and so on)? What, in other words, beyond the development brought to cosmopolitanism in intermediate Stoicism (Panetius, Posidonius and, after them, Cicero), does the Roman period add to the question of the universal blocked in its contradiction with the singular? Isn't it precisely that it begins to find a solution to it using the junction sketched out between these different levels, those of the universal (as a formal notion) and the common (as a political project)? In fact, in the way Roman citizenship sprang up, the two meet for the first time: its juridical status, on the one hand, in the mode of an imperative [*devoir-être*] and not being able to tolerate exceptions, defined a necessary prescription which had a universal value; and, on the other hand, the sharing of this citizenship was progressively extended to the point of rendering the 'Roman land' common to the whole Empire, without further exclusion. The importance of Rome is thereby to have united the two under the same legal bond: the 'City State' and the 'world', the *urbs* and the *orbis*.

Rome therefore provided Europe's first experiment in a globalization which went beyond the wide-ranging uniformization of customs (togas, thermae, the circus, the games, the harangues and so on), which inevitably proceeded from the cross-fertilization of populations and the circulation, on such a vast scale, of goods and ideas. Along with the status of *Roman citizen* a single institutional and legal form was superimposed on the diversity of places, peoples, morals and religions. Supported as it was by the figure of the Sage alone, the appeal to virtue and fusion with the cosmos, the world-city of the Stoics remained more a moral than a properly political concept. In Rome, in contrast, 'universal citizenship', *universa civitas*, begins to become effective: in law, the universal emerges from philosophy and from its logical seed so as to define a unity of status and condition. This juridical status of citizenship is then distributed, little by little, from the Italian municipalities, from the last centuries of the Republic to the first ones of the Empire, through remits that became more and more immense, decided as a whole and extended to the most distant territories: those which were bordered by the *limes* and thereby designated the end of the habitable, or at least integratable, world. With the Caracalla edict in AD 212 this citizenship was finally conceded to all of the inhabitants of the Empire, as though it was really a matter of a necessary evolution. Thus, the *a-priori* exigency of the one (the universal of prescription) and the extensivity of the other (the common of sharing) finally managed to join in this institutional form of Roman citizenship, before the jolts of invasions overturned it.

2 A characteristically non-exclusive Roman conception of the common has often been invoked (and recently in an intelligent way by Claudia Moatti (1997)) to explain this capacity Rome had for absorbing so many diverse histories, peoples and sparse lands into a community which seemed to be unlimited – for military success is not sufficient to account for this prodigious extension. The evidence for it is in the founding narratives. Rome incarnated a spirit of opening *ab initio* which radically opposed it to the principle of the restricted, and even fiercely private, community of which the Greek cities were so proud. While the citizens of Athens entertained no doubts about their noble origin (since they considered themselves to be born as 'indigenous' from that very earth and drew pride from their ethnic longevity), Rome was happy to recognize itself, on the contrary, as a 'jumble of strangers'. Whether we trace its foundation to Aeneas and therefore to Troy, or believe the city was established by the Greeks, and whether we still consider it to have a barbarous origin, Rome has no difficulty in admitting (as is, moreover, common sense) that

the *urbs* was born from immigration and that it experienced mixing from the very outset. Indeed, under cover of the story of Romulus and Remus, it avowed that it was peopled at the beginning by bandits and fugitive slaves who came to seek sanctuary on the Palatine Hill. They were, as Titus Livius says of the first Romans, an 'indistinct mix of free men and slaves, all of them seeking something new' (I, 8, 4–6). Indeed, far from wanting to conceal this, to say the least, questionable origin, Roman historiography stressed the positive aspects of such a composite foundation that allowed Rome to develop.

There were no limits, then, to Rome's expansion, since the essence of the Roman, strictly speaking, arose neither from soil nor from blood. In any case the identity of a city was not, from the point of view of the Romans, of an ethnic nature; far from being a stain, the mixing of populations constituted, in their eyes, an advantage. In the same way, while Greek thinkers associated the perfected character of their city with its limited nature (*teleios*, as first predicate of the *polis*, linked by Aristotle with the idea of perfection to finiteness), the Romans did not themselves envisage any termination of their growth. In a different way from the Greek cities, Rome discovered, through what was nevertheless its imperialism, its syncretic vocation: by absorbing so many foreign, especially Oriental peoples, it would compensate for its youth with their antiquity, and thereby take support from their past age. The ideal recognized by those who, already in those days, looked into its astonishing destiny is less to have sought to conserve (the identity and the specific: a pure blood, original cults, an ancestral language . . .) than to have known how to *integrate*. The native welcomed the transient element, or profited from it, and in its way the rape of the Sabines illustrated this marked tendency for adoption. Indeed, Rome took no pride at all in being first and barely claimed originality at source. Its opening, favouring its indefinite extension, was on the contrary based upon what has been called, so as to characterize the 'Roman way', its principle of 'secondarity' (Rémi Brague, 1992). Without false modesty, the Romans recognized themselves as descendants and not pioneers. Rome imitated, borrowed, absorbed; it adopted and adapted; it developed, as did its language, by successive accretions. For, rather than seeing this continuous influx as a threat, it knew that it would be enriched by it. In spite of what often appeared to be clever propaganda, which its periods of oratory gladly served, it has to be recognized that Rome founded its *societas* on a new connection: no longer of a segregationist nature, whose purity would be defended, but rather, effectively, of 'association', resulting in the establishment of a common world from shared traditions and ideals.

3 But Rome was remarkable not only for having enlarged its frontiers to this extent and pushed back its limits so far. In this new age of globalization, it is exemplary for us not only because of its capacity for integration which, over several centuries, allowed so many diverse peoples, races, languages and cults to cohabit. Rome most certainly teaches us a lesson in being a successful melting pot. More instructive, however, is that in the end it knew how to link one and the other: to embed this territorial and civilizational extension, favouring the *common*, in a unique legal status (Roman citizenship), and so founding *universality*. The question then becomes one of whether this should be understood within a frame which would now be juridical rather than philosophical. As recent work (notably that of Yan Thomas, 1996) has shown, and contrary to what has too often been reported about the 'concrete' spirit of the Romans, such a diffusion of Roman citizenship outside of Rome could not have been carried out other than by the construction of a very elaborated and even astonishingly abstract law.

> For, as Rome did not conceive, by developing and conquering the peninsula, of a territorial (Italic) State as such, one that would be normative – homogeneous, in other words as it did not actually think of itself outside of the physical frame of its own city, the new civic community formed by the colonies and the Italic municipalities could not be conceived of except by means of a *fiction*, that of the 'homeland commune', according to which the territory of the City incorporated that of the other localities. One thereby found oneself, even though a citizen of some other city, at the same time being permitted also to be a citizen of Rome. With juridical construction substituted for the reality, this principle of a 'ubiquity' of Rome led to a legal homeland (*patria juris*) being established everywhere else, which would then be superimposed upon any local sense of belonging. The citizens of cities external to Rome

thereby found themselves Roman citizens on the same basis as if they had been living in Rome itself. Thanks to this casuistry, one found oneself Roman while remaining in one's own (local) homeland. And one continued to be in one's own land when one journeyed to Rome . . .

In this way the celebrated distinction established by Cicero assumed a rigorous institutional meaning and led to the two being juxtaposed in a theoretical complementarity (*De legibus*, II, 5): the lesser and greater land, one 'natural' and the other of 'citizenship'. As was said of Cato, 'he was Tusculan by origin and Roman by citizenship', and one possessed at the same time a geographical country and a legal homeland: the first is where we were born while the other has 'welcomed' us. But the latter must reign over the former even in our affection, because the name of the 'public thing' becomes in its example, Cicero proposes, that of a 'universal citizenship', *civitas universa*. It was therefore in Rome that the *community* began to *universalize itself* in a positive way through the law. Not only did it extend to the limit of the frequented space, but it also acquired a formal status which was presupposed to be rational, the source of all obligations and arbiter of legality. With what constitutes a Roman being no longer given but constructed by means of the juridical connection, 'Rome' ceases to be limited to an individual and concrete city on the map, but is now the 'second mother of the world', *parens mundi altera* (Pliny, *Natural History*, XXXVII, 201-205) and becomes a unique space, abstracted from geography and born from a new consanguinity, that of all the citizens of other cities gathered together by the same, equally protective, civic law, in the *civitas romana*, now *maxima*.

Hence arises the idea we see celebrated by the Romans themselves: that, in uniting all people under Roman law, by revealing to them a common land, Rome, putting the finishing touches to nature, has given mankind *humanity* (withdrawing it from its 'immanity': *immanitas*).[1] The Greek separation between Hellenic and Barbarian vanishes. Even before having recourse to the distinction between two lands, the local and that of right [*de doit*], the *De legibus* posed in a logical way, as a preliminary condition for this civic universality, the unity of the 'human species' (Cicero,

I, 28-33). As a notion, it no longer triumphs by being concretized, as in Plato, but is now central and rests on a principle of natural equality. It resolutely lends itself to the character of universality which takes it back to its definition. It raises 'man' to abstraction and so 'Whatever definition one gives of man, it is unique and valid for all' (while 'if there is difference in the species, a single definition would not grasp all individuals' (I, 28-33)).

Admittedly, Roman citizenship, in the age in which Cicero was speaking in this manner, barely extended beyond the Italian municipalities. Nevertheless, thanks to the law, the logical universality of the definition of man, whatever the content, already carried within it the principle of an extension of the common as an internal requirement, even though centuries would have to pass for it to be ratified by History: 'It therefore follows that nature has created us to share with one another and place the law in common among us all' (I, 28-33). The law has actually become the stable base, the recognized guarantee, of humanism, at least in European culture, and it was under these conditions that humanism was actually formulated in Rome, as Cicero incarnated it, rather than in Greece. For all that, we know that it couldn't reign alone like this for very long – for it could not remain linked to the destiny of a City State opening out in an unlimited way under the auspices of its protective gods and representing the world. Indeed, in the same age and in this same Empire, it would fall to Saint Paul – by appealing not to the law but to faith, and who wanted, by taking apart every statute with a view only to salvation – to reverse this formal universality of citizens. In so doing, he sought to substitute for it another universality which would be capable of affecting the intimate life of subjects even in its most singular destiny. This would therefore occur without any further addition to the membership of the group, as Cicero's citizenship demanded, but rather by abolishing it.

VII Paul and the matter of going beyond all communitarianism in Christian universalism

1 Therefore, from what other logic (or should it rather be called anti-logic?) did the universality that Paul promoted by preaching the Good News brought by Christ effectively draw its strength at the other end of the Roman world? This strength was above all born from a reversal. Free to benefit from that vast environment without frontiers, unified as it was by language and morality and by the principle of right which Roman expansion had produced (which also served its diffusion), Paul's evangelization took its power of renewal from what it openly confronted and claimed to dismiss, the most imperious thing in this world: the law. He who had, by rallying to the Pharisees, first been its intransigent defender, suddenly turned against it. Against the whole prestige of the law, both Roman juridism and – above all for Paul – Jewish legalism, the mission the apostle assigned himself was really to show that a universality of salvation could only come about by supplanting it. This is the justification for slicing into History and introducing a new reign into it: 'Christ redeemed us from the curse of the law' (Galatians, 3, 13).

For, in spite of the formal absoluteness its statement confers, what does the law, any law, actually hold us to in the particular?[1] Not only, as has so often been said, because, when they are compared, laws are diverse, and indeed they contradict one another; not only because they are devoted to this plural – the laws – and they distribute their commandments and specify their conditions; but especially because all law, as a principle, through the regime of obligation and retribution it instigates, imposes a prescriptive mode of determination that overwhelms all others: it deprives itself of so many other possible modalities. Under cover of taking up every case, it encloses within a univocity which is that of constraint and summons. Its logical regime is that of predicative affirmation alone, from which it is unable to emerge. Therefore Paul sets up 'grace', *charis*, opposing it to the law. *Grace* names precisely what exceeds any possible predicate and, in contrast to the law, it does so without having to. From the outset it overflows any narrowing of projected links and their causation, and even points towards their inherent illegitimacy. Hence it opens a fresh horizon for the universal, one in which there is no longer anything which is preconceived.

Or, if Paul does refer to a law, it is to that 'spiritual law', *nomos pneumatikos*, in which the regime of obligation is seen to be struck down by something disinterested, which he names 'love' (*agapé*). 'Love is the fulfilment of the law' (Romans, 13, 10). By completely 'filling it up', properly speaking (as *plerôma nomou*), he dislodged law from its empire, putting an end to its validity. This results in a major transformation: 'love' defines this law as anti-law, one which is no longer either plural or literal, and which, un-specifying relations, renders the commonality [*commun*] of sharing absolute and *living* ('death' being a withdrawal into the particular). Hence, love is the bearer of a connection which has ceased to be formal, as in the law, but it includes from the start the personal destiny of all people, who are touched in their private lives. The uniqueness of Love thereby allows them to be raised up as universal subjects, each of whom nevertheless continues to be unique and singular in the way that as individuals they are open to it (such is the major contribution made by Christianity, which from that moment will combine these oppositions).

For, at the root of Paul's teaching and as something which is continually inspiring it, there really is this paradoxical truth: that the least believable statement is by that very fact accessible to everyone. On the one hand, it is less dependent on justifications which are always taken into the web of particular notions and arguments: the most incredible statement is one that is the most liberating. On the other hand, the most 'crazy' statement is the most universally credible, because it places all people on an equal footing in their identical difficulty in believing it: at the foot of the same wall of faith – of the same scandal of the Cross. That Jesus might be resurrected, which is the basis of all of Paul's teaching, is the statement that is most available to the free conviction of each person, because it gains least support from the contiguous truths assumed in the constructions of various classes or cultures; it operates as an abstractor of all particularism (emptying it out), making the path clear for a new condition, one freed of the heritage and allegiances of the past. In obliging a break with knowledge born of repetition and anonymous experience (that of 'mortality'), it forces us at the same time to extricate ourselves from weak generality, which is confined to observations, so as to project the truth onto a completely different level by ostensibly cutting ties with the *doxa*. It compels an emancipation from the regime of ordinary attachment, which is largely passive because it is split up into the diversity of beliefs and opinions, so as to transform it into an act of voluntary, explosive, and thus mobilizing, adhesion which would be absolutely the same (unique) for all believers.

2 In preaching the folly of the Cross, Paul thereby promoted universality in at least three ways: he most openly detached it from all belonging (from milieu, language and community); most radically forced transcending any cleavage (of Jews and Greeks, or elected and excluded, and so on); and finally he constrained all subjects to relinquish any individualizing plenitude of opinion and position, so as to gain access to the internal destitution demanded by faith. It would then only be through faith, and not by works of laws (Romans, 3, 27), that the Christian message would be rendered equally accessible to all people, making them all one. The first operation, of *detachment*, can itself be recapitulated under a three-part heading. For, from the outset, this major fact has to be taken into account: that, although contemporary with Christ, Paul nevertheless did not know Christ. I mean that he did not know him personally: he neither lived nor spoke with him, he never even met him. Christ did not have particular features or a face for Paul, who could not act on any direct anecdotal particulars. Freed from the familiar and from any physical proximity, *de visu*, and from its sinking into the circumstantial, the intimacy Paul maintained with the Lord is not attached to the narrative (what is more particularizing than a narrative?): it was necessarily of another order. As for all people who came after him, it was an intimacy that could be secured only 'spiritually'.

> Equally striking (and revealing of the way in which Paul conceived his teaching) is that Paul went off to teach the Good News to the nations strengthened by the revelation that came to him alone (on the road to Damascus). He did not therefore first of all go to those who had been the direct disciples of the Lord to enquire among them: he would wait three years before going to

Jerusalem to meet them. The knowledge Paul sought concerning the person of Christ was consequently not of the order of information, which is always localized. Paul had no interest in learning anything more of the details or the reported facts and actions of the Lord, since the only thing that mattered to him was the economy of salvation as it encompassed all times in a single event. Free from everything anecdotal, Paul could carry his message in a purified state, that of death vanquished and the new Adam. Nothing biographical, or even hagiographical, would then emerge to cast the enunciation of the incredible truth back into the particular. This message, from the outset taken away from any particularity, seized people in the irreducibility of their condition and was addressed to them all.

The second feature which detaches Pauline teaching from the human anchorage in Christ and his mental ground is to be sought in language. Christ expressed himself in Aramaic (even if he had probably been in contact with Greek milieus) while Paul spoke (and thought) in Greek. Paul thus freed the Christian message from its native word. He released it from what a language (any language) contains in its specific articulations and possibilities, and took it beyond itself through the test of alterity: to emerge from the implicit understanding that a language maintains with itself and, hence, to dissociate it from its idioms. So not only did Paul translate his message but the translation, by transferring its content according to other, notional and syntactical, expectations, crossed the frontiers of the source language, taking its universalization with it. It changed not so much the language as the language family (from Semitic to Indo-European). It was even more striking that, speaking Greek, Paul at once switched the Evangelical message into that language within which the universal that is the *logos* of the Greeks, detached from its mythic gangue, was intended to be expressed. If he openly asserted the very opposite of Hellenic 'wisdom', Paul nevertheless benefited from all the work it had done to release an abstract and conceptual level from the singularity of the phenomenon and the empirical. By raising this opposition to this wisdom, he at once elevated his teaching to its intellectual level. In this way the message from one sect (like so many others that existed during that period, and did so more or less in a thaumaturgical way) flowed into the language developed to articulate the rational constraints of truth. In other words, if the well-known scene of the Learned Assembly (Paul engaging the philosophers of Athens in dialogue) is false and paints too simple a picture, it can no less be justified. In encountering the Greek and the demands it made, the Christian message changed description. Not only did it benefit through the use of the medium of the most widespread language employed from one end of the Roman world to the other, something which thereby favoured diffusion, but it also found this resource in it, making it more comprehensible (from which the Septuagint had already benefited): exploitation of the language of philosophy.

The third form of detachment of Paul's teaching in relation to its original conditions and limitations, carried along by the two preceding ones, was that of his own effort and continuous battle: the fruit of a lifetime. This was no longer precisely one of abstraction (in relation to the story of Christ and his language), but rather of extraction, the *extraction* that Paul carried out little by little, since it was so difficult and perilous to put it into effect outside of the Jewish community and its law (even if he had in a certain way been preceded, in this consciousness of a universal mission, by the Hellenistic Judaism to which he belonged). For, no matter where he disembarked, Paul could not begin his preaching anywhere other than in the synagogue: as a Jew, he began by addressing Jews. But his teaching then caused this frame to burst open (most often he was thrown out). In fact Paul was conscious of the danger of everything that would fix the News into a communitarian place and prevent it from spreading universally. Similarly he feared the communitarianism (or exclusivity) that any community bears within itself. When Paul finally went to Jerusalem, the question which could not be avoided in the relationship between Peter and Paul was really this: to what extent did the new doctrine have to remain dependent on the milieu which bore it? Paul did not have the slightest intention of giving up his position. Against the idea, supported by the disciples in Jerusalem, that Christ had come to accomplish the law but not to bring it to an end, Paul supported the contrary view that the rupture introduced into History by the coming of Christ abolished the earlier signs or, worse, rendered

them irrelevant. In other words, if the new truth is really dependent upon a tradition ('for the Jew first and then for the Greek':
Romans, 1, 10), the universality to which it accedes nonetheless
breaks with all affiliation.

Through these various operations constituting a sort of breaking open
of the seal, Paul proposed to neutralize the differences so as to leave the
level upon which faith was to be raised uniformly smooth (and equal).
There was no longer anything but a single affiliation which, dissolving all
others, was that of man in God. Any cleavage (of race, sex or condition)
is to be abolished. This was because everything which would set up an
obstacle to the universality of the Announcement was to be superseded.
A sentence from the Epistle to the Galatians (3, 28) expresses this revolutionary shift: 'There are neither Jews nor Greeks, there are neither slaves
nor free men, there is neither male nor female: for you are all one in Jesus
Christ.' With the effacing of the distinction between Greeks and Jews
also goes that between the two discourses Paul established as opposing
examples to make them the doctrinal alternative of the Ancient World
(I Corinthians, 1, 17-18): those of integration (through wisdom) and elec-
tion (through the message); or the one who argues against the one who
prophesizes; or the one who demands proofs against the one who expects
signs; the one who reveals to man his place in the order of the universe *or*
the one who deciphers the promise of salvation in the history of a people;
that which is founded in reason or that which prevails through the status
of the exception. It therefore follows that, henceforth, 'there is no distinction between Jew and Greek' (Romans, 10, 12). In the same way, in the
regeneration of baptism, to which all are called, the distinction between
the circumcized and the uncircumcized loses its power of inclusion and
becomes null and void (Galatians, 6, 15). Paul maintained this against
Peter so as to blow open any measures of exclusion by which Jewish
communitarianism intended to differentiate itself (this at the time of the
dispute in Antioch around the question of meals taken in common with
non-Jews: Galatians, 2, 11). Or, if he left separations in place in the realm
of the temporal, between man and woman, master and slave, at least he
abrogated them before God. No longer would any category have the
monopoly or even simply the privilege of Union.

3 Nevertheless, the question arises (as soon the Christian episode would become immersed into its world) of what distinguishes this Pauline disregard for the diversity of conditions from what Stoic cosmopolitanism (based on the largely vulgarized Stoicism which we know influenced Paul even in his art of the diatribe) had already developed in the debris of the cities. For that also equalized different positions. But it did so only through a removal of frontiers and an increase of scale, in a perspective that had become 'cosmic', that of a natural world that was understood to be governed by reason. While this Stoic egalitarianism proceeded through the abstraction and reduction of contingencies, for Paul the surpassing of separations between people relied upon the fact that they all exist only through and in the same filiation with God, who is no more the God of one than of others, no more the one of the Jews than of the Pagans (Romans, 3, 24). Humanity itself is therefore one, not so much through a community of nature as because, ever since the Creation, it has been committed to the same history (of the Fall and of Redemption) which sealed for all time the divine plan of salvation but which Christ had finally come to reveal. This unity opening onto the universal is therefore not only that of the divinity and its providential design, but also that of the announced Event. This occurred once and for all and for all peoples. The resurrection of Christ (the victory over death) is the pure and absolute event, freed from anything anecdotal (but, even so, not symbolic) and absorbing all others into it. In fact, these are of no concern to us, not because, as Stoicism proposed, they now embrace a causal necessity which escapes us, but because there is only a single event which counts – a causeless event, accorded through grace, through a 'gift' (Romans, 3, 23) – which, as soon as one believes in it, changes everything. It holds its universal significance due to the fact that it dismantles within it all positive histories and that, overhanging all spaces and all times, it pre-empirically imposes upon the whole of humanity, as is effectively required by the concept of the universal, the necessity of that which is from that moment reduced to the same condition that dissolves all of the others: that (unique) condition of children of God all equally promised resurrection.

Let's therefore take account of both: on the one hand of the fact that the only consistency of which humanity would be capable unfolds from its complete dependency in relation to a single God who is the same for all people; and, on the other hand, of the fact that the same Event, vouchsafed by God and proclaimed by his Son, would alone be constitutive of human history. From this unfolds a complete *hollowing out* of the Christian subject which no longer possesses anything in its own right, anything which is due to its own nature: this subject, liberated from all specifying determination affecting the subject in itself, is what is most radically open to universality. The Roman subject, as a subject possessing rights, was a full subject, one anchored in natural determinations (of birth, origin, rank, family and so on) from which it had to take care not to remove itself, at the same time as there would be superimposed over them the formal universality of its *civitas*. But the Pauline subject has rid itself of all features other than that of the Event of Christ and its filiation to God. The universality which returns to the subject does not accrue to it by right of supplementary attribute, but results from the equal nudity (the nullity without God) of what has effectively ceased being for the subject a nature properly speaking (since it is lost), and is only an Expectation (an appeal) staked in all times as a collective destiny. Every person is eternally this same empty form which God alone fills up. So from the outset this negative (hollowed-out) identity alone sweeps away differences and renders people identical to one another: there is only the void which would be absolutely identical (to the void) . . .

The result of this is that Christianity has profoundly modified the form of the universal: it underwent a transformation which revealed to it a new future which paradoxically links it to the singularity of the Event. Instead of opposing itself to the individual, the *hekaston*, as Greek reason imperatively constructed it, it now conjugates itself with it in the person of Christ – of the God made man and *incarnating himself*. On the one hand, God is the pre-existing *Logos*, 'before all worlds', and participating in every respect in the divine absolute; but, on the other hand, the Word is made flesh, 'and dwelt among us' (John, 1, 14); he lived, sorrowed and suffered like everyone and underwent the experience of the various ages of life. Following Paul (from Justin to Irenaeus of Lyon, from Origen to Augustine commenting on Saint John, and so on), the teaching of the Church Fathers was really to bring the two together. The incarnation of God in human history, from the birth to the resurrection of Christ, is the inscription, at the heart of the singular, of a universal Love. Dissolving the contradiction between the two, rather than resolving it, Christ conferred the form of a logical reconciliation on salvation, and it was certainly to this that Christianity owed, in part, its force of conversion. At least this was so in the realm of philosophy. Through his extended arms, as he was nailed on the cross, 'he led the two peoples dispersed at the extremities of the world to God'; 'But in the centre there was only a single head to show that there existed only a single God, above all, in the midst of all and within all' (Irenaeus of Lyon, V, 17, 4).

4 We know only too well how this form of the concrete universal has since then passed from the religious into the European interpretation of History (to which Hegel ultimately subscribed): great men, each one in his own time, being the organs of the substantial spirit of their age, therefore consistently realize within themselves the 'true relation of the individual to the universal substance' (Hegel, 1953: II, 2). On the one hand, 'the universal they have accomplished, they have drawn from themselves', such men labouring and struggling from one day to the next in their particular way to bring about their ambitious design by their own efforts; but, on the other hand, this design, which might be thought to be borne by their egoistic interest, 'has not been invented by them' because it has 'existed for all eternity' in the as yet unrevealed Spirit, even if it was through them that it was realized and 'found itself honoured'. The Christian paradigm has barely faded. As the *great man* has known how personally to implement this new form of the universal by means of his relentless action, although it has barely risen above the confusion and particularisms of the age, he is the one through whom the idea of salvation has been converted into Progress. Thus the individuality which belongs to it becomes that of the Concept, revealing through him the singular path of its development, and it stopped at European civilization, then at its apogee thanks to the proven success of science, no longer than to design at will, and for the rest of the world, the forms of this incarnation. It did so by transferring this vocation of universality, by secularizing it and using it to name its modernity by means of it, to new candidates.

Already the Church, 'Roman' in its conception, had once more encountered both the universal and the common, just as Rome had

already done. By calling itself 'catholic' – in other words by appropriat-
ing the logical concept of the universal (the *katholou* of the Greeks) – it
had shown how what is still historically (empirically) only a community
or particular 'assembly', a 'church' (*ecclesia*: that of the baptized), could
attribute to itself the mission of exporting the absolute truth it recognized
(prior to all human diversity, since it was addressing itself to all people
and transcending all time periods) everywhere throughout the world,
through converting by force and rarely by will. Paul, the apostle of
nations, was really the promoter of this as he ceaselessly founded communities and worked to spread the Good News 'to the extremities of the
earth' so as to open the path of salvation to all people. But how far would
the Church go in this direction? For, confronted with the differences
between cultures, faced with the resistance of other cults and beliefs, the
Propaganda of the Faith of which the triumphant Church had made its
historic calling was no longer content to carry its message ever further.
Rather, it rendered this message resolutely irreconcilable and, devoting
itself in this way to the impassioned eradication of any other conception,
seen as the vestige of 'superstition', it finally assumed its universality
from the sort of *exclusivism* with which all commonality [*commun*] is
threatened.

A phenomenon such as Christianity, which has known a historical success lasting for so many centuries, cannot thereby be explained
without considering how it judiciously took advantage of this operation,
that is of the fact that its soteriological message, very common among
many sects, was recognized and denounced as 'madness' already in Paul,
because of the requirement whetted by reason; and it could not therefore
save itself except by putting together (and forcing through) the universal
as something completely disconnected from the variety of experiences
and opinions. As it did so it nullified them all so completely that it was
thereby able to monopolize belief. Then, with the Church of Bossuet and
his *Discourse on Universal History*, in which the universal, it seems to me,
creates an intersection between what he largely considers to be planetary
and the prescriptive of Truth in a way that is decisive as it reconciles
profane history with sacred History. This vocation to lead humanity on
the march is seen to transfer, beyond the Hegelian function of the great
man and through a systematic declension of possibilities, no longer to a

religion but to a people (again in Hegel), to a class (Marx), or even to a civilization, which would be its own (the 'Western' one). This is how the West would have *incarnated* within itself alone the necessary development of Reason and how it would thereby extend the springing up of universal values for the whole of humanity.

VIII Does the question of the universal arise in other cultures?

1 Such a progression was imposed as a starting point and point of access. It had to begin with a reconnoitring of a lot of the various entry points before committing further to this massif of the universal that is so precipitously dominant today. For I do not see how it would be possible for us to grasp this question of the universal, in the way it now overhangs the relation between cultures, without initially investigating where we stand in relation to it. This 'where' is manifestly as ambivalent as could be. This investigation therefore needs to start by striding along its mental ground, recognizing the terrain from which it has been formed, and tracing its genealogy which, in leading us from religious prophecy to political institution, deliberately bursts out of the philosophical field (in this respect aren't Paul or the legislators of the Second Century of the Empire as important as Aristotle?), or, rather, without, in this very field, examining what its *geology* would be. For we acknowledge that this great folding up of the universal, so that from then on it would haughtily dominate thought, emerged from multiple pressure points which to begin with had no relation with one another, and they have brought with them some astonishingly disparate materials, even if it is just a matter of these three pressure points persisting: the concept – citizenship – salvation. It thus has to be admitted that our thinking about the universal arises from a dispersed – or in any case not centred – history, one that is composite, not to say chaotic, and which is sedimented in a succession of levels whose formations remain, to say the least, heterogeneous when considered in cross-section.

And, strictly speaking, is it even possible to compose *a* history from it? For, if these three aspects are our only concern, what link which responds to these pressures, each of which has its own logic, could there be between them: the demands of the *logos* as it responds to the necessity for determinations appropriate to science, the juridical constitution of 'double citizenship' that responds to the needs of Roman expansion, or the apostolic invitation to go beyond all human divisions that responds to the unique vocation of 'God's children'? . . . How far are these various sequences able to be co-ordinated or even simply to meet one another? Do they constitute anything other than juxtaposition and overlap? Or do they at most buttress one another? Evidently there is nothing here from which to compose a 'history'; there is only an accumulation and concentration of demands through a superimposition of layers and a stratification of pressure points.

It no less remains that thinking about the universal has benefited from this accumulation which has contributed to making its foundation even more solid. Penetrating into such diverse terrains has enabled it to draw the appearance of a plinth upon which the constructions of philosophy have consequently (but acting as though it began with a blank slate) erected it. It has surreptitiously increased in transcendence from the crossing of so many layers. This has occurred to such an extent that it has succeeded in concealing its inherent ambiguity under considerable unanimity and we see classical reason, in principle so anxious about foundations, halt its establishment at precisely this level. Indeed, in spite of its heterogeneous construction, the universal is projected as a keystone and a unique aspiration. In spite of, or rather *because* of? For this arrangement of lenses, layered as it is, is convergent. To return once again to those three levels: the elevation of the concept, borne by *logos*, has made this universal the end of abstraction and even of the work of thought; similarly, the political expansion of the Roman empire supported the extension of the law which was then turned into the objective of the community; similarly, the emptying of any subject as it responds to the appeal of God has made it the destination of the soul and the objective of humanity as a whole, and so on.

This leads me to wonder whether European ideology was not born, at least in part, from this visual effect: from these successive levels, with their diverse pressure points which, even though they had no relation to one another, were aligned by the universal. Not that such a universal could have steered their design in combination, still less could it have ordered them together, but through it alone these heterogeneous (philosophical – political – religious) levels reveal a perspective in which they have just a little in common, furnishing them, for want of further interlocking and penetration, with a valuable meeting point on the horizon.

For where else, in an ideological context as unfocused as that of Europe, could an articulation on such diverse levels be found, conferring as it does some cohesion or at least coherence upon them? Hence the universal has prevailed in European thought by having this status as an aim, drawing every ideal to it (does it even allow any others to survive?) and constantly haunting modern consciousness as it seeks a continual incarnation. Henceforth it becomes a global exigency, and because of this is one that is above suspicion, which means that its locality comes to be forgotten, even becoming global today, since it has been definitively hypostasized while imposing its imperative [*devoir-être*] in the realm of values as much as in that of knowledge. It is what, more particularly, has ordered the necessity of Reason and the development of History according to the same enfolding, and so has made its triumph the ultimate aim of the human race.

On the threshold of the modern age, a painting like that of *The Adoration of the Mystic Lamb* by the Van Eyck brothers already gives an image of this teleology of the universal monopolizing and saturating representation. At the two upper extremities of the polyptych, Adam and Eve come to us, no longer cast down under the effect of Original Sin but extracted from human history, naked and expanded, indeed magnified and promoted to the sublime level of the divinity, since they bear the destiny of humanity as a whole as promised by salvation.[1] In the same way, responding to the Virgin no longer represented as a simple mediator but as queen of the heavens crowned with stars, John the Baptist raises his hand to bear witness to the total Trinity: the customary representation by which he points with his index finger in order to indicate Christ's coming is no longer sufficient. In just the same way, the central representation of the Lord enthroned in majesty in his pontifical clothing superimposes Christian symbols and those of the Old Testament so as to incarnate the Almighty in a single form. Each individuality represented therefore systematically reflects the same universality of message, which is both abstracted from History and definitive. The same thing is also true for the lower panels: under the dove and the rays of the rainbow illuminating celestial Jerusalem, converging from the four corners of the world, towards the Fountain of Life and the altar of the Lamb, are 'crowds of all nations, all tribes, all peoples and all languages' (Revelations, 7, 9).

These cohorts of the blessed are the most explicitly diversified, down to the flowers on the lawn: Virgil mingles with the patriarchs and we can make out in the background a Chinese hat. But all of these figures participate equally in the blessedness of a paradise in which the sky, no longer being contrasted with the earth, is split into these two superimposed registers. Forming a univocal vision in which, from one end of the horizon to the other, bringing time to an end, and *a priori* leading everything to it, the ultimate is perceived (conceived) and even imagined. From now on, nothing is hidden.

In the way in which it makes all culture and all thought converge towards the revelation of the same truth, subordinating all belief and hope to the same demand, one will have no difficulty in reading the Van Eyck painting as the first apotheosis of the idea of universality. Admittedly, it's easy for the iconography, when these panels are taken to the laboratory, to show the multiplicity of layerings and re-paintings – indeed, that the actual whole has resulted in its arrangement 'from an ingenious ordering of heterogeneous elements rather than from a pre-determined and unified project' (Panofsky, 1953: 205). Throughout his analysis, Panofsky insists on this contingency. But isn't precisely the same thing true for the idea of universality? In the same way, was it ever preconceived and predetermined? It has equally been layered from diversity and has continually superimposed the heterogeneous and even the motley onto it. But, as in the Van Eyck painting, you only see the effect of totalization and alignment after the event, opening a unique perspective and resulting in all of its composite nature being forgotten.

I can no longer conceal the unease I feel each time I consider the Van Eyck polyptych. I mean to say that this is an ideological unease, but it is one for which no aesthetic pleasure can compensate (since in it the art of representation also turns to saturation – the two go together), and which I must immediately emphasize does not stem from the religious motifs I have evoked. What is disappointing is this *a-priori* monopolization of what is thinkable as it runs through each motif and representation, extinguishing all contingency under cover of universality, at once blocking growth and subsuming every possibility. In this panorama of Truth, any tremor of indefinition is stifled from the outset. At least it will no longer be possible, when viewing this painting, to fail to ask oneself at least two questions. First, have we seen another culture form a similar aspiration? (In other words, can we find an equivalent of the *Mystic Lamb*?) This leads us to this initial enquiry. Is the preoccupation with the universal itself universal? Or could it be a theoretical phantasm, even if an eminently productive one, which the West alone has forged – one that is therefore amazingly singular?

And in a similar way we can ask: has any other culture correspondingly sought to project its values onto the rest of the world, arguing for their universality and with a view to converting the rest of the world? Or, on the contrary, have they considered their values to be particular to them, and have either not dreamt about the universal, or been satisfied with their singularity? This will lead me to a further questioning which, after some hasty incursions through other civilizations, is close to my heart: couldn't we then conceive (but how?) of another modality of human universality? Not just one which distrusts any message, even the best-intentioned one, but one which equally refuses to be overawed by meaning and even any logic of convergence and rallying: that precisely of a universal which does not aim to saturate all possibilities, but on the contrary works as a *desaturator*, reopening from what is lacking in each positive formation–institution, so disturbing their legitimacy, and leading them back into a risky distance which shuns the convenient reassurance of any fencing in.

2 Wouldn't Herodotus be just as much a Father of Philosophy? That is, before Socrates, who we know was something of a homebird and hardly ever left Athens. For is there another way out, at the point at which I have arrived, and even if it means failing in the purely conceptual play of philosophy, apart from that of giving oneself over to an 'enquiry', a *historia* in the proper sense, as Herodotus was first to do? Wasn't this moreover already the figure of the daring Ulysses? In other words, going 'to see the world', meeting with other cultures, exploring their resources, questioning their traditions and conceptions, something which all in all recalls the initial meaning of the *theoretical*. Before this term served only to express contemplation of the mind and the choice of the speculative, these missions and voyages undertaken abroad were called 'theories'. We read in Herodotus (I, 30) that Solon was called a 'philosopher' – and this may perhaps even be where the word is encountered for the first time

– because he travelled to discover the world: 'because of theory' (*theôriès heineken*). But philosophy has since denied this origin. It has stayed at home, has ceased to venture, and balks at such work of enquiry, considering it impure.

From now on I believe that it will no longer be possible to dispense with it; that, after such a long withdrawal which has led to it enclosing itself (dogmatically, or rather endogamously) in its own history and filiation, philosophy finds itself once more forced into it. Not through simple curiosity and comparativist pruritus, or to use and even expand its knowledge, or due to good-conscience/good-will, or because today other cultures increasingly and vociferously demand their own originality, and so on. But rather because of the internal limits it today discovers in its own practice and which constrain it from re-envisaging the universality of which it has boasted. This is because, in developing its own options, and even if it has constantly gone back over them and re-worked them, to criticize them, and therefore, by so doing, to transform itself, European thought still finds itself caught in certain configurations of the thinkable which as a result close off others, and so it can therefore conceive of this *possible* elsewhere of thought *only from itself*, in spite of all the repeated unfoldings to which it has ceaselessly and with so much passion devoted itself.

For as long as we remain within the heritage of Greek thought, the question of the philosophical status of the universal has to be raised. It is imposed on the mind as a logical question and every theory of knowledge is obliged to pass through it. All that is needed as proof is what we discover, in close proximity to Europe, in the Arabic tradition. Not only does this return to the debate opened by Plato and Aristotle and their commentators, but we also know that it carries the dispute about universals in new directions which the scholastics did not fail to borrow, in this way forging, in the half-light, the questions and concepts which the European philosophy of the classical age will later luminously put into operation.

> As it did so, taking over the conflict of realism and nominalism, between those who conferred upon the universal a status of reality separated from the perceptible and those who conceived of it on the contrary as the product of an abstraction operating from it, Arabic philosophy pursued the analysis not only according to the

themes, but equally according to the *folds*, of Greek thought: the opposition of the empirical and the intelligible, of the perception of the senses and the intuition of essences, of the various sorts of intellect, and so on. And it extended the distinction carried out between the three types of universals: those which are *prior* to the multiplicity, such as in the mind of God, as intelligible beings (1); those which are *in* the multiplicity, by way of being physical (2); and those which are *subsequent* to the multiplicity, by way of logical beings, such as those conceived by our minds (3). Henceforth to cleave in a clear way, as we were already obliged to do, between the stage of the shared, 'instantiated', *in re*, universal which is that of the common, on the one hand, and that of the abstract universal, of which we no longer even ask if it actually exists, on the other hand (see Libera, 1996: 177s).

Nevertheless if, moving on from Arabic logic, we turn towards the Islamic religion, don't we already see a certain limitation, or relegation, coming into focus in relation to the universal? Or, let's say: a lesser interest? In any event, it has to be admitted that, if the thinkers of Islam were passionate about Greek logic, this would not be the case when it came to ethics; at least, the bridge built by the European Middle Ages between Aristotelian morality and monotheism, promoting the assimilation of the Supreme Good, or Bliss, to the vision of the divine essence (on which Thomism constructed its universal) still appears to have barely been sketched out among Arabic thinkers (see Vadet, 1995).[2] The question, once the Christian paradigm was installed, was not so much to know whether the universal remains the supreme value, drawing the whole of human history to it, and completing it (because Islam evidently remains under this paradigm, as much by its strictly unitarian conception of the divinity as by the final scene of Judgement embracing the whole of humanity), but rather: is the religious predication in Islam also conceived *according to* the universal, in other words, subject to its demands and with a view to propagating it? Or are these various pieces of data, of an ethnic, linguistic and juridical order, and so on, maintained through the message, singularizing it in this way as of right, without compunction or even simply suspicion of what appears *to us* (by 'us', I mean contemporary universalist ideology) to mark a limitation?

Having consulted my Islamicist friends about this, I will first of all note these two points of divergence. On the one hand, in the case of Islam (differently from the Gospel – Christ speaking Aramaic but the Gospel being written in Greek), such a detachment from the source language has not taken place, and this incontestably protects its idiomatic character. Thus, the News of the Revelation was not presented and did not gain influence in a language other than that of its initial predication. Even if the Arabs have later translated many Greek texts, the religious message remains in Arabic and does not appear disturbed by the fact: from the outset it has not submitted to the universalizing test of translation. Indeed, the first verses of the Koran, upheld in everyday prayer, can be recited only in Arabic. On the other hand, Islam remains attached to the idea of the prophet, and he continues to be associated with the idea of a people and therefore of a particular place. The prophet is of his tribe. Admittedly, he is commonly called upon to renounce it in order to be more effectively recognizable apart from it and to return to it later in triumph, as Mohammed did. All the same, each nation has had, has or will have, *its own* prophet, for such striking truths cannot be pronounced except in the language of those concerned. In contrast, the fact that the divine nature of Jesus, making him without distinction man and God (which in the end was what Islam would deny to him but which would be inscribed at the heart of Christian dogma), intentionally takes Christ out of the tradition of prophets and abruptly separates him from any ethnic belonging, from the outset conferring upon his teaching a universality which, through its transcendence, incommensurably overflows any human perspective and restriction.

When it comes to religious teaching properly speaking, I see in what Islamicists have taught us at least two major reasons that have led Islam to develop *some interest* in the universal. The first is the importance of obedience to the *sunna*, which is the custom consecrated by the Prophet and the first representatives of the community. Doing good works would therefore not be conceived in a notional way (and we know that Islamic morality has a marked aversion to abstraction), but consists in conforming as strictly as possible to such venerable examples, the science of the religious coming to merge with that of tradition: at any hour of the day, even the smallest details of existence find in it a model to be observed, as recorded by jurists, such a legalism starting on every occasion from the particular so that in each case how to act can be deduced through analogy. The law is not therefore purely moral in essence; it is also a positive knowledge, developed even in the simplest actions that are still crucial for the reward of salvation. If this law equally demands to be loved and needed for itself, like a very dear memory of the most precious heritage, then it cannot, for all that, have the universalizing character of love, which is indifferent to the particular and tends to confound everything at the heart of a common aspiration (moreover we know that mystics, in Islam – those in whom Europe has been so interested – will continue to be just a little suspect here). Obedience, in effect, is necessarily specific and is formed of distinctions, being understood in a detailed way, item after item; while love (to which all of Christ's teaching returns: God is love) logically dissolves the whole of this particular, melting it in an equalizing and undifferentiating movement which at once carries it along and abolishes it.

The other Islamic limitation brought to the universal would be contained in the priority accorded to the community which, as we know, has, as a rule, two faces: one of sharing but also one of exclusion. On the one hand, indeed, the fact that the communitarian duty might be considered the principal requirement in accordance with the *sunna*, or that acts would consequently have value only in relation to this communitarian spirit revered as the norm of everything, makes such a community (*uma*) the pre-requisite of Islamic consciousness. Then, on the other hand, this community, in Islam, is one founded by the Prophet on the basis of institutions which, in their inherent simplicity, are at once religious, moral and political. It is that of the only nation on earth to have received the privilege of the *sunna* and the one whose triumph is awaited; it is founded on a pact of solidarity (*walâya*) which, uniting man with God and excluding any other belief, is also that which has been sealed on the battlefield and that we see rouse the holy war, which is not, for all that, conducted with a view to conversion.

The motif of the neutralization of all markers, posed by Paul as a principle (neither Greek nor Jewish, neither slave nor free man, neither male nor female), was thus abolished in Islam (the slave can be freed, but we know the fate reserved for women even in the hereafter). In Islam even the history of salvation, a universalist theme if ever there was one, remains inscribed within the particular optic of prophetism and its expansion on the earth. It remains strictly individual and does not arise from a global economy as did the one introduced by Christ, that of the new Adam. From this perspective, Islam links back on the whole to Judaism, with Christianity between the two, going rather on its own way through its universalist inspiration which marks out the community of the Church from its terrestrial inscription; this, moreover, corroborates both its connection with Greek philosophy (through the patristic) and its separation as a principle from any particularizing, territorial or political institution.

3 The example of Islam thereby steers us towards making a start on separating these two levels: on the one hand, logical universality (which we find highly developed in it) and, on the other, the universality of values, which we perceive no longer to be the decisive factor as far as its community is concerned – this retreat and this lesser extent being understood in relation to Paul's universalism. Wouldn't comparing them constitute Europe's originality, the fact that it claimed to have aligned one of these over the other, the latter over the former, superimposing them to the point of wanting to identify them? Envisaging thinking of action in accordance with the formal universality of knowledge and endowing the moral law with the sole rational, self-founding, necessity of logic– Kant being the prime example of this. Even if it generally comes as no surprise, as it begins with this *doxa* that hereafter emanates from global information, it becomes historically important to make this clear. Didn't it constitute a hardening characteristic of European thought as it purified morality of everything not arising solely from the requirement universality made in being raised to an absolute not only of thought but also of behaviour? And didn't this mean that it had to be purified of anything arising from ethnic belonging or from sex, age, birth, social status, tradition and so on? Comparatively, the case of India, if it is looked at in parallel, makes this European exception stand out more clearly still, as it detaches social ordering and implied ideals most obviously from all logical universalism.

Indianists in fact teach us that India has developed a certain idea of the universal (notably in the Nyaya-Vaisesika current) and it has done so, as is the case of all logic, by opposing the fact of having a common feature (*samanya*) or a similar property (*sadharmya*) or, in a vaguer way, some resemblance (*sadrsya*), to the particular (*visesa*). The universal is thus defined, in a generic way, and with a view to operations of class, as the unity which is the cause of the identical conception of particular things, subsisting eternally in each of them, even though this perception of the universal necessarily depends on the perception of the particular to which it is inherent. Is there, for all that, any debate and discussion about universals in anything like the same way we encounter it in the West? The comparison has recently been attempted in India itself but, let us note, in English and therefore already according to European categories (see Raja Ram Dravid, 2001). Is this therefore sufficient to prove that its ancient thinkers had made conceptual abstraction the departure point of their thinking, as was the case with Aristotle? In spite of possible transpositions and cross-references, did their reflection develop *according to* the same demands? For we know that the adherence to the world in India has remained such that one cannot stand back from it, and that no break occurred there between the intelligible and the perceptible. Consequently what place, between *perception* and *Revelation*, could it keep for the deployment of the concept? Madeleine Biardeau reminds us with great pertinence about this important distinction: the notion of the universal and of logical necessity may fail at the very moment it is handled. Thus it was possible for conceptual and not particularly complex mythic systems to develop in India without, for all that, having an explicit and definitive idea of what a concept is or of its operative (legislative) power in relation to things (Biardeau, 1964: 141ff.).

On the other hand it is incontrovertible that the caste system blocks any ethical universalism in India. For it is impossible not to take preliminary account of the four classes or 'colours' which compose Indian society, from that of the Brahman reserved for priestly functions, guardians of 'Brahman' culture and, consequently, of the social order, passing through princes and warriors (*ksatriya*), by way of agriculturalists and traders (*vaisya*), to that caste, at the bottom of the scale and subservient to the others, which no longer has a share in the rituals and is considered as external to the perspective of Revelation (*sudra* – not to mention the 'untouchables', on the boundary between the human and the non-human; or even women, since to be re-born a woman, even in a Brahman family, is still a form of atonement). Not only is this structure hereditarily (ritually) hierarchical, but it especially introduces divisions which, as a principle, are impermeable at the same time as they are inherent and which fragment moral thought according to so many distinct states, the individual himself being identified with his social function and existing only through it. In a village, there are traditionally two wells: one for the pure, the other for the impure. There is no conception or ideal which can transcend this process of belonging. The *dharma*, as global and cosmic-social order, as established from the first cosmogonies, consists in respect for this inexorable distribution (and repetition) and cannot be the same for each of the groups: these serve as a frame of identification (and not simply of specification) for any elaboration of values.[3]

Would seeking to evade this functional partition and its compartmentalization even so put it on the path of a universal? For the response will be that there is certainly the contrary aspiration in India, and above all among the Brahmans. This means that the Absolute is sought outside the social group by those who, no longer satisfied with the values of the world and having rejected its rites, aspire to escape from the spiral of vicissitudes, of deaths and rebirths and so reach the point of being re-absorbed into the undifferentiated (*Brahman*), thereby acceding to 'deliverance'. Yet it is still the case that such a deliverance, in the first place, can be understood only within the framework of the superior classes, or *varna*, and most particularly of the Brahmans. On the other hand, at the moment when the 'renouncer', *sannyasin*, separates from the group, an individual act par excellence, this would not be in order to affirm his individuality more strongly but, on the contrary, to abolish it. By abandoning the world, he abandons at the same time everything which made of him an *ego* in order that he may melt into the Absolute. Therefore the universal also disappears, since any singular determination with which it would be in tension and would work, and without which it cannot therefore exist, vanishes, and any consciousness itself fades as deliverance approaches. In this state, there is no further place for the constitution of some level of ideality onto which the universal could be projected, nor even for any totalization or absolutization of meaning (since life from that point on has no 'meaning'). This radically distinguishes such thought, and in a definitive way, from the Van Eyck polyptych. This should also serve to remind us that the universal has pertinence or is understood only as an operator of an imperative [*devoir-être*]. What is in view is not a renunciation, but a surpassing (of singular limitations and restrictions) and it is in the service not of a re-absorption-confusion, but really of a promotion, a promotion of essence, justification and legality.

Islam has conquered much but has not, for all that, sought to convert. In India the situation is striking. Born Hindu, one will bear this belonging, in addition to that of one's caste, in an indelible way, without any possible going beyond it, this belonging itself having no meaning outside of the Indian context and the *dharma*. Not that this dharmic order is limited to India or might know some provisional limitation, since it is the cosmic order, but it is nevertheless only understood, in the eyes of Hindus themselves, from an Indian perspective, in an autochthonous way, and only within the fold of its sacred texts and tradition. Thus India considers itself apart – *sui generis* – and does not conceive of exporting its 'values'. Its caste system (or the escape from it) is not of the order of a position of truth (which could be discussed or proved, attacked or defended), but is perceived as an immemorial given which, as such, could be exposed not to rejection, but only to denial. It no more assumes that it can be contested in its core than it is concerned about not being recognized elsewhere. Inversely, to claim to elevate anything at all to the universal is not only to remove it from its sense of interdependency, but also to promote it to the ultimate state of truth. Thus the universal bears within itself, as an intrinsic requirement, the duty to export itself in order to assume its imperative [*devoir-être*], and it has constantly needed to convert since it has regarded any non-recognition of it as an intolerable challenge to its legitimacy. Such is really the history of Europe.

4 As distant as these worlds of India and Islam are from one another, they are still close in this respect: they both rest on a global order (Islamic, Brahmanic) at once invoking a Revelation (the Koran, the Vedas) and recommending themselves to a Tradition to which it is understood that the whole social body adheres. This constitutes an endogenous understanding, if I dare express it thus, and one which does not even need to be justified – to seek to escape from it, rather than criticizing it, still evidently implies this attachment. As it gains sufficient cohesion to safeguard itself against dissention, how could such an ideological order therefore concern itself simply with what might come to contest it externally? Founded on Ritual and Law, this unitary order is inseparably 'religious' – 'moral' – 'social' and 'political' (according to divisions and categories which are those of Europe alone), informing, at one and the same time, personal conceptions and communitarian ways of life. Taken as it inevitably is into a history, it nonetheless closes itself off from all historicity, crediting itself with a pre-established continuity. Even 'philosophy', far from claiming to be itself an autonomous discourse and practice, would mistrust being innovative (which of course does not mean that it might not be), developing in the shadow of the religious without finding anywhere it could radically move away from it or definitively dissociate belief and thought from one another (to keep to these Greek concepts of *pistis* and *mathesis*). Thus these cultures nourished a feeling of belonging that was strong enough for them not to have to consider either being removed from their indigenous source, or an external takeover that would unify a scattered ideological multiplicity. They have no need to forge a convergent stress point that would at once be justificatory and would transcend their disparity. In other words, they *do not need* to pose the question of the universal, at least apart from having to have the technical skills necessary to shape their knowledge in a logical way.

However, tempted as we are to introduce other cultures in their turn only so as to frame the fate of Europe alone by confirming its exceptional status to our own advantage, will we ever be adequately on our guard against that facile Hegelianism which constantly re-emerges in European thought? Does it not itself thrive on the illusion born of distance, leading us to neglect, through ignorance, the internal mutations and diversities it contains from elsewhere? Or couldn't Europe in fact have had a different heterogeneity regarding the internal constitution of various cultures, of which it constituted an extreme case, something already easily apparent from afar and forming a standard? When it comes to the universal, I can see myself reduced to returning to the outlined hypothesis. Europe has had a much greater need to valorize the universal due to the fact that it was constituted from various impulses, ones which did not have a great deal of relation between them, and which remained in a state of tension. Or, to return from this point to the question whose urgency is emphasized ever more clearly by the cases of Islam or India, in their contrasts: what link should therefore retrospectively be assumed between those disparate products (if we just restrict ourselves to these three – those of the Greek concept, Roman citizenship and Christian salvation)? With demands being born from different (philosophical/political/religious) horizons and on different levels, which themselves hardly tally with each other except through the idea of the universal, which they each claim according to their own particular modality, and have even more and more strongly themselves tended to empower (from which stems the ambiguity with which this idea remains marked), would span these driving forces in tension at the heart of European culture and discover a possible intersection or reconciliation in them. Being unable to blend and integrate into a common conception (as even Thomism was unable to do), didn't they find a point of convergence and rallying there?

This, then, enables us to extend the hypothesis proposed. Doesn't the universal (which is cultural, concerned with values) create itself only when the ideological unity of a culture is insufficiently strong, forcing it to erect this stress point or ideal focus, an extreme form of its transcendence, in order to remedy this weakness? Thus, while medieval Europe had no need to promote the universal outside of its logic, the influence of Christianity at the time being sufficient to assure its cohesion as at once religious, moral and political, the question of the universal surged back unabated in the modern era which, having lost confidence in Christianity and neither seeking nor finding a substitute for it, experienced a lack of ideological integration and discovered something with which to re-establish some coherence only at the daring extent of its thought, of promotion-postulation – this 'lack' (of ideological integration) which moreover should be understood, it seems to me, less as a defect than as a fertile negativity, such as has precipitated its history.

5 Let's consider a final representative case: to complete the typology, that of a culture which boasted of no Revelation, but whose power of ideological integration and re-centring is nevertheless such that it has placed itself at the centre of the world and held its values to be unrestrictively imitable, as well as indefinitely exportable. It *has not even* posed the question of their possible universality. Such is the case of China. Or rather, in order to illuminate one through the other, let us consider these two cases of China and Japan: converse cases, but neither of them has taken the trouble to pose the *question* of the universal. In one, this cultural universality is self-evident; in the other, it is incongruous. In Japan there has been no interest in it because Japan luxuriates in its locality and requires it. It calls upon it in its insularity, in its climate, its earthquakes, its narrow plains and indented coastline (*fudô*, *yamato* and so on). It is land protected by the gods, living on the fringes and with a unique destiny. Having to recognize its cultural dependency towards its great reactive neighbour, far from cutting into its feeling of internal adhesion, reinforces this identitarian awareness through continuous confrontation. From the point of view of the Japanese themselves, Japan is a culture of the singular; the question of the universal has nothing to say to them.

In contrast, extending from its great rivers and vast plains, China encounters only the marches of its empire and sees nothing more in it than peripheries – except the sea. It perceives itself to that extent to be a culture of the global, something from the outset which it considers self-evident. And it has no need to produce a concept of the universal in order to proclaim it. The space it attributes to itself is nothing less than what is 'under heaven' (*tian xia*); it unfurls 'inland from the four seas' – in other words, goes to the ends of the world and its sovereign extends his power over the whole human race. 'The Son of Heaven is unequalled', they say of him: no one is matched with him; indeed, 'between the four seas, no one can receive him according to a ritual of hospitality', since everything 'under heaven' is 'his house' and there 'is nowhere for him to go that is outside' (Xunzi, beginning of the 'Junzi' chapter). Thus, 'no matter what frontiers he crosses, no matter what the lands to which he goes . . . it cannot be said that he is returning, since he is at home everywhere' . . .

In the most ancient collection of poems of China, the *Shijing*, we can already read: 'Universally under heaven / there is nothing which is not the land of the King' (*Xiaoya*, 'Bei shan'). What is translated here as 'universal' (*bo*, replaced later by *pu*) signifies 'that which can encounter no limits' or is 'indefinitely spread out': not, properly speaking, claiming an imperative [*devoir-être*], but nor does it conceive of any reservations about its point of view. The hyperbole of the expression does not indicate the invocation of a necessity but the non-suspicion of any possible alterity (or exteriority). Not in fact authorizing any sacred word, therefore not proclaiming any Message, not being founded on any Grand Narrative, ancient China did not consider itself as pre-destined, nor even simply privileged; it was just the only civilization that was (re)cognized, and as far as it was concerned everything that surrounded it had not yet reached the same point: it had not yet been 'made Chinese'.

For around the 'principalities of the centre' which constitute it (*zhong guo*), so many peoples and various tribes (the Yi, the Man, the Rong, the Di) are distributed, each filling its place, according to the cardinal points (to the East, the South, the West and the North) and each of which has their separate customs: they may not knot their hair, or they may tattoo their bodies, or they do not cook their food, or dress only in skins, or do not eat seeds, or live in caves, and so on (*Liji*, 'Wangzhi', I, 1). But what, more importantly still, distinguishes them in all respects from the Chinese and leaves them in this condition, blocking them in this state of pre-civilization, is that they are without rituals. The 'rituals' (*li*), as the Chinese understand them, are not reserved either for a people or for a caste, but are the behavioural norms 'channelling' desires and linking the internal qualities with civilized forms of conduct. As such, they extend their empire from one end of our activity to the other, from the sphere of the sacrificial to that of politeness, passing through court etiquette and propriety (once again, our European separations of the religious/political/legal/moral are mingled together). Fitting every circumstance of life just as they adapt to each degree of the social hierarchy, and therefore being 'globally' valid so as to ensure the regulation of the world, they assume no restriction to their adoption. Other peoples, not yet being civilized, are simply awaiting this acculturation. Mencius (III, A, 4) states: 'I have heard of men using the doctrines of our great land to change barbarians, but I have never yet heard of any being changed by barbarians.' And there was a time when the Master (Confucius), no doubt disappointed one day by the lack of success his teaching was having, not without humour, proposed that he would go to live among the barbarians of the East: no matter how rough and primitive they might be, he replied to those who objected, 'if a single good man', a civilized man, a gentleman, would establish himself there 'would they still remain rough and primitive?' (Confucius, IX, 13/14).

China has therefore had no conception of universalism in a theoretical way – that is as *a-priori*, separate and prescriptive – but in a civilizational and 'humanist' way that, as such, doesn't have to separate anything that would transcend it from experience, at least not in a radical way. It has therefore been led to envisage it categorically neither as a logical universalism producing the concept, nor as a juridical universalism enacting the law (there are in China no 'norms' (*fa*) of recompense and punishment), nor as a redemptive universalism, at once the most incredible and the most open to all, as it requires the same brutal rupture of the Faith of each person, as well as levelling nations, types and conditions. But it gives it 'nature' (*xing*), in which all people have their origin, as a foundation. In this sense, Confucian humanism is revealed to be in close affinity with the pre-Christian Latin humanism of Cicero. Indeed, should we be surprised, since the two of them aim less at constructing and detaching a level of ideality than at getting support from the manifest work of civilization alone? Moreover, they both belong to two empires and two ages, at the two ends of the great continent, where a culture believed it was possible to extend itself indefinitely over the inhabited or at least urbanized world which was protected by its frontiers (*limes* in the one case, the 'Great Wall' in the other), without encountering the resistance of a true alterity and due simply to the fact of its institutional, moral and political power.

For both men, the crossing of differences is of such magnitude and extends on such a vast scale that it allows them to think about human unity. Confucius said that 'People are close by nature (*xing*), but are distanced from one another through practice' (XVII, 2). This is exactly what Cicero said (*De legibus*, I, 29) opposing *natura* to the fold of 'habits', *consuetudines*, and developing the same idea of a vocation of man taking root in the order of the world and contributing to its promotion. But, while Christianity in the West covered over this civilizational humanism by abruptly opening up the human vista onto the absolute of the Message and the universal of God's plan (of salvation), in China, in contrast, this humanism was disturbed by no Revelation (not even by Buddhism as it came from India). It knew no Narrative other than that of its own history and it had been able to cross the centuries, up to the end of the nineteenth (until the arrival of the West in force), without being disturbed – its world was complete, moral and physical at the same time (the two not being dissociated), itself obeying 'constant rules' which it possessed in an intrinsic way (Mencius, VI, A, 6, citing the *Classic of Poetry*; see Cicero, *De finibus, passim*). Humanity thereby *naturally* forms only a single community whose vocation is nothing other than to cultivate this very humanity ('the alliance of the human species in its entirety', said Cicero; or 'Between the four seas, all people are brothers': Confucius, XII, 5).

We then understand that the Chinese, just like the Latins, were notably not very enthusiastic about a purely logical universal. Why would they have had to turn from experience to found the universality that their civilization, in its springing up, had allowed to appear of itself on another level (of essences)? In this civilizational perspective, the operation of knowledge also consists, in China, in going from the 'local' to the 'global' (*yi qu/da li*, Xunzi, beginning of 'Jie bi'). This is not letting one's vision be obstructed by a 'corner' or an aspect of things but to embrace them in their totality. For, once the distinctions of types and species useful to the classification of knowledge were established, the Chinese had no interest in disregarding them to extract from the multiplicity of the diverse an ideal unity founding a pre-established necessity; but they aspired to deploy their vision of things so as to render it coextensive, as far as is possible, in space as well as in time: 'Sitting in his hall', the Sage 'sees everything as far as the four seas'; 'he knows the warp and woof of Heaven and Earth and regulates the ten thousand beings', and so on (Confucius, XII, 5). To reach this state, there is no need for an intellectual asceticism relinquishing the sensible and being elevated to the abstraction of the theoretical, but it is useful first of all to render one's mind available by means of 'emptying it out', 'concentrating' it, and 'soothing' it, for it is only when it is not burdened, over-extended or disturbed that it can reflect spontaneously on the configuration of things and be able to know 'equally' (without further 'partiality') everything that exists.

> Extensive management of the general is opposed to competence limited to the particular. 'Even if he is in complete possession of his profession as a farmer, a peasant could not be Director of agriculture; or even if he is in complete possession of his profession as a merchant, a trader could not be Director of the market; or even if he is in complete possession of his profession as an artisan, a worker could not be Director of the craft industry.' It is then other people who, without being experts in these branches, can ensure that they will be well administered. They are experts when it is a matter of the 'way', *tao*, and not in a given material; instead of being confined themselves to a particular management of the particular, they elevate themselves to the perspective of the whole (Xunzi). It is here, in this call to pass from one level to another, that such a development could recall the beginning of Aristotle's *Metaphysics* lauding the surpassing of the empirical through the universal and causal knowledge of 'art' (technique) and the theoretical. Then, on the contrary, we perceive in it precisely how the thought of the *tao*, the 'way', as thought of the viability of things and their integrated functionality, blocks the development of abstraction. For the unity which relates to the *tao* is that which crosses and links internally the multiplicity of things and situations (which therefore cannot be grasped except under intensification of the gaze, see Confucius, IV, 15), but not that which would be erected in a unitary form of representation (as universality of the concept). This is why the ambition remains here that of the management of the world, as a work of civilization, and not that of a pure project of knowledge: a world of lettered functionaries – *guan*, 'function', concludes at this point – and not of philosophers.

IX Are there universal notions? A cultural universal having ideal status

1 Will we after all that be held to this outline and initial signposting? From the point of view of the 'enquiry' engaged in, *historia*, the question of the universal is still to be grasped from another side. The fact that the demand made by universality might not have been developed and reflected upon in other cultures as it was in European culture is not sufficient to call its relevance and legitimacy into question. The question is overdue and flows back from that other side: wouldn't there still have been universal notions, which could be encountered as such at the base of all cultures, even if other cultures have not thought about (and abstracted) the mode of universality? These might be, so to speak, established notions at the root of all human intelligence, constitutive of the very work of thought: in the way by which we, as people, *all* people, *a priori* become aware of existence and necessarily represent things – these are what structure the human mind. As such, it is logical that we will find them in one language as in another. Thus there are 'Being', 'truth', 'time', and so on.

As it is considered that such basic notions and representations *could not fail* to be present in all cultures, at least in an implicit way, they will be called not only common (from the point of view of sharing) or general (due to the fact of extensive observations which will never be contradicted), but properly (strictly) 'universal', since they imply an imperative [*devoir-être*]. It is necessary, in an unconditional way, and without it even having to be verified, to pose this pre-established necessity – universality; it has an axiomatic status. Otherwise, we would run the risk of jeopardizing all communication and comprehension between people: of jeopardizing, consequently, all humanity. Considering everything that is involved in this debate, which is not simply philosophical but also, much more broadly, moral and political (wouldn't leaving this universalist position mean immediately sinking into relativism, which is not only always internally inconsistent but also ideologically deviant, tipping over into neo-colonialism, or even worse?), it appears from the outset to be preferable to cut straight to an affirmative reply: to put a halt to the discussion there, to institute a certain safeguarding measure or clause (humanism) by fixing this safety catch against risky speculation. Let's shut down the construction site because it threatens to be impracticable, and in doing so stick to what is prescriptive . . .

Besides, if we would like to override these protests, what could we hold on to that would enable us to tackle the question? For when we think from, through and *nestled within these notions*, and due to the fact that we lack virtually any distance from them, how would it be possible for us to introduce some reflexivity when considering them? Nevertheless, this is where I believe sinology can furnish a unique support. In effect it provides such an external point of view – I will repeat here once again its conditions as it amazes me that they have not yet become more visible, that such a *methodical* use of China has not undermined philosophy's self-contentment. For Chinese and European thought have developed independently of one another for such a long time that their two worlds did not communicate (except in a very indirect way, in relation to material needs, through the Silk Road). As a matter of fact, they were completely unaware of each other until the sixteenth century (when the first evangelical missions disembarked in China, though they would have little influence) and for the most part until the nineteenth century (with the imposed opening of Chinese ports and the beginning of forced Westernization). On the one hand, the two languages, those of the European and the Chinese, are alien to one another, something which was very different from the case of India which was able to communicate with Europe through the Indo-European language (Greek and Sanskrit having the same grammatical roots and categories) and, on the other hand, no historical relation of influence or contamination can be inferred between these worlds – very different again from the Islamic or Hebrew worlds which had been engaged in a continuous cultural exchange with what would become Europe: the Koran integrates Jesus as a prophet and the European Middle Ages rediscovered Aristotle through Arabic translations.

At the same time, China was a world of thought just as developed, textualised, clarified and commented upon as ours in Europe. Placing China and Europe in relation would therefore be on an equal and symmetrical basis (quite differently from the dissymmetry in which anthropologists operate when they take as their terrain populations which have remained separated, have not developed writing, and are almost without history). Overall, because it is pure or not suspect, China furnishes an ideal case study to use in order to test the universality of those 'basic' notions we consider to be self-evident and by means of which we think. Indeed, we cannot actually think in their absence – even if we may return to them so as to challenge and criticize them, we still cannot ever *imagine* being uncoupled from them – and we pose them from the outset as 'universal'.

So let's return to some of the notions I have already had occasion to tackle in my work in order to learn something from them. With this in mind, let us consider the notion of 'being' from which Europe, from the time of the Greeks (ever since Homer), initially constructed its thinking. 'To be' or 'not to be' form its logical but also dramatic alternative par excellence, just as the opposition of Being and becoming (*einai/gignesthai*) constitutes its line of cleavage from which ontology developed, the royal road of philosophy. Then, just as we would be unable to think outside of this fold of Being (which is where our thought articulates itself), we are conscious that being is expressed 'in several senses' and above all those of existence ('it is') *or* of predication (to be such and such or in such a way). Do these meanings converge towards the same unity (*pros hen*, as has been defended from Aristotle to Lesniewski) or do they remain completely alien to one another, in this way becoming the source of confusion? (Russell: it is a 'misfortune of the human race' to have chosen to employ the same word 'being' for two uses as different as predication and identity (quoted in Kahn, 1973: 4)). But, to be precise, is what is really at issue here the 'human race' or is it rather something expressly Greek, which 'we' in Europe have inherited? Classical Chinese speaks separately of 'there is' (*you*) or 'as' (*wei*) or 'existence-subsistence' (*cun*) and equally it knows the copula function (*ye*). But it does not express (does not think) Being in the absolute sense (*haplôs*, as Aristotle said) – that is, being as 'type', that in which all other types must participate if they are to be called 'beings' (Plato already said this in the *Sophist*); or that of being 'as being' (*on he on*) and from which philosophy, ever since Aristotle, must be science. Chinese thought has not been able to pose, or more accurately *has not had to pose*, the question which for us has nevertheless until now seemed to be inevitable, that of the *ti esti*, or 'what is it'?

Instead of contenting ourselves with responses of supposed 'common sense', ready-made responses which, given from the outset, are reassuring for us, it will therefore be appropriate to commit ourselves to a prudent and patient analysis which henceforward ceases to be purely a matter of sinology, but entails a decisive importance for the comprehension of our own thought and its possibilities. Where are we then with 'truth'? China has actually thought about circumstantial 'appropriateness' (*dang*, notably among the Mohists) but, because they have not been able to prop it up with Being, or to establish it at the level of eternity, or to support it with a pure project of knowledge (tending, as with the Greeks, to assimilate wisdom to science, *sophia* to *epistémé*), but in contrast have accorded the primacy to what we call so restrictively in Europe 'circumstance' (*quan*; see Confucius, IX, 29), they have not constructed Truth as a major aim of philosophy – the 'has not been able' here certainly not being the expression of a lack, but the opening up of another possibility (see Jullien, 1998: 95). The term in classical Chinese that could be best translated by 'true' means rather 'authentic' (*zhen*: in the sense of true sentiments or nature; the 'true man', *zhen ren* is, especially in Taoism, the one who has known how to gain access to a perfect internal availability and no longer experiences any stumbling blocks to the flowering of his existence). Or the Chinese have effectively handled the disjunctive judgement: 'it is this' / 'it is not this' (*shi/fei*: true or false, good or evil), but, once their schools of thought were formed in Antiquity, they soon challenged the loss which the (sterile) conflict of positions inevitably occasioned (and which Zhuangzi never tired of denouncing), from the point of view of the 'globalism' of wisdom (of the harmonizing plenitude of the *tao*). What this meant was most certainly not that the Chinese have been unable (or have not known how) to distinguish true from false, but that they have not developed their conceptions *from this perspective*, that of the Quest for truth.

There is already something in this to trouble philosophy. Something is problematic about our received evidence, which begins to force the dividing line between the universal and the singular to shift. And that also comes with a warning. In order to enter into Chinese thought it will be advisable to follow the development of its notions and questionings without pre-supposing that its modes of coherence agree from the outset with the ones we have in Europe. Let's abandon this naïve representation: on the one hand, we have no universal notions and, on the other, there are cultural variations in them. For not only will our great philosophemes not be found as such on the Chinese side; equally absent will be even those notions that seem among the most general ones, those we might think were 'invariant', like that of 'time'. I have previously had occasion to show that the Chinese had conceived, on the one hand, of the 'season' (the moment – occasion – circumstance: *shi*), and, on the other, about 'duration' (*jiu* – coupled with space, including among the Mohists), but not the notion of a homogenous abstract time, detached from the course of proceedings, in the way the Greeks conceived of it by starting at the same time with a physics of movement of bodies and their displacement in space (Aristotle) and with a metaphysical rupture with the eternity of Being (Plato – Plotinus) or of God (Augustine); and in the way that we ordinarily fold it into conjugations marking different tenses – the Chinese language does not conjugate (see Jullien, 2001: chs. 2 and 3).

> Would this be the same as saying that the Chinese have had only an implicit notion of it, as has been proposed by sinologists unable to admit that the Chinese might not have had this 'universal concept' of time? But why then would they not have developed it? And could their thinking about processes and the transitional have blocked it? Or wouldn't that by contrast bring about the emergence of what in Europe is still enigmatic and paradoxical in the thinking about time, something it has constructed and enthused about: its 'obscure' existence, as Aristotle says, since it is 'divisible' (between various times) but whose divisions do not exist, the present being only a moment of passage, without extension, therefore without existence, between the past which is no longer and the future which is not yet? The proof of such a divergence, in any case, is that, when they encountered Western thought and science, at the end of the nineteenth century, the Chinese and the Japanese needed to translate the Western notion of 'time' ('time' being then translated by 'between-moments', *shi-jian* in Chinese, *ji-kan* in Japanese). The same thing goes for the

difficulty of translating 'being' or the 'ontological', or the 'truth', or the 'ideal', or the 'will' and so on, something that at times is still debated today. At the same time, let us remain attentive to this fact: when, as is so often the case in a Western translation of classical Chinese, we encounter the terms 'truth', 'being', 'time', 'ideal', 'will' and so on, it is not evident that the Chinese terms should be translated in this way. Rather, an assimilation has already been effected, so as to cast the foreign meaning more effectively into our language, making us *already* retreat into the mental frame of its possibilities and our theoretical expectations. In this way the illusion of universality is generated cheaply but unjustifiably.

2   The fact that all translation might be betrayal, as is commonly stated, does not in itself say everything. Confession or concession, the formula remains insufficient, for the question is not simply one of fidelity (which one may have lacked). To translate, especially between two languages and cultures which are unaware of one another, we enter into that risky zone, one of approaching silence, where what we convey as evidence of our thought is suddenly rediscovered, in the mirror of the other, caught in a mesh of strange choices; just as we will never gain, in the midst of this disturbance, an external point of view, an overview or even as little as a step back, allowing consideration of both at the same time. We are either in one language *or* in the other – there is no back-language as there is no back-world. This other language – other thought – forces us to stand back from our own, but so as to make us tip over immediately (or more precisely we have already done so) into the network of the demands it makes. There is no *medium* that can hope, in other words, to be 'between-languages' – 'between-thoughts'. This means that the question of translation comes back to that of the universal. As soon as we cease to believe, in a simplistic way, that a provisional correspondence exists between cultures, how will we be able to conceive of the 'passage' between them?

If we can't count on the *invariants* delivering a *given* universality to us, we will propose to recuperate it by finding or producing *equivalents* from the other side. Will this equivalence, from one culture to the other, then itself be assignable? We already know that it cannot be direct, that the more pregnant the notions in collective thought are, the more they find themselves caught in a perspective which is elaborated by language or by its use, from which we cannot remove them and therefore would be unable to transpose them. I have previously taken as an example, in classical Chinese, the term *ʒhen*. If I translate it by 'true', as is usual, then in doing so, soaked in the European bath, it becomes something completely different. It immediately coagulates within it a desire for knowledge (or at least allows itself to be contaminated by this cumbersome proximity) which no longer has anything to do with Taoist detachment – indeed, it is what Taoism challenges above all. The same thing goes, for instance, just as much for 'Heaven' in the *Zhuangʒi*, in which it means not some pre-established Exteriority, in relation to our world, but rather the world's absolutely natural and unforced course. And when it refers to 'celestial food' it expresses not Manna but the vital nourishment which clears everything away, constricting, by way of external stimulation, the renewal of our vitality (see Jullien, 2005: ch. 4). From this, one will be constrained to re-work such a notion of equivalence by conceiving it not so much as analogical, founded on resemblance and cross-reference, but as *functional*. In other words that the representation encountered on one side will be made to undergo all the necessary transformations and reformulations (*mutatis mutandis*, says the standard formula) to the point that it meets with a problematic of the existential order which plays the same role, on the other side, and might at least be able to take its place in a certain way.

There is a major stake which is more than a mere example. Indianists inform us that we would be unable to find a direct equivalent in India of the notion of human rights that Europe has posed as a universal. But if we put this European representation through the required mutations and reconfigurations, then because of that necessity, without which it would not have a true universality, a corresponding representation will necessarily be found in Indian culture (see Raimundo Panikkar, 1998: 221). It will thus be necessary to seek what, within Indian culture, can satisfy an equivalent 'existential need', especially by asking how the representation of a 'just social and political order' can be found in it. I would make two remarks about this. First of all, would a wider representation, when released from the merely European horizon (that is, from what we are told would be a 'just social and political order'), even then succeed in assuring the transition in an effective way? In other words, has it submitted to enough necessary modifications and unfolding for that to occur? Or, rather, are the loosened levels of the 'social' and the 'political', as well as the notion of 'justice', still marked by a conception specific to Europe? Could one extend the formula farther and yet still retain some meaning? On the other hand, I notice that, once these considerations of method are established, precisely when Raimundo Panikkar turns to India to consider what might effectively be the concept of human rights there, he is unable to do anything other than enclose himself in the notion of Indian *dharma*, which we know to be indifferently cosmic and human as well as indelibly marked by which caste one belongs to. Consequently he is not really capable of making it communicate with the European notion, posed as it nevertheless was at the beginning as universal. When put to the test, submitted to the requirement to fit into Indian conceptions, the quest for such a cultural equivalent, even a functional-existential one, reaches a dead end.

> It's not that we foresee that finding a way to establish a communi-
> cation between cultures, even between those that have remained
> alien to one another for so long, might prove to be impossible.
> But I believe that it is first of all appropriate to assess the extent
> of the misunderstanding that is inevitably introduced between
> them, indeed which can be commonly (ingeniously) maintained,
> as soon as we think we are able to establish a correspondence
> between notions without considering more fully the particular
> perspectives in which they are inscribed on one or the other
> side. Let's consider for example this notional disjunction of the
> 'there is' / 'there is not', as it presides in the thought of the *Laozi*
> (*you/wu*). Will we find any difficulty in giving it as a functional
> equivalent of the opposition between 'being' and 'non-being', one
> that assumes an analogous importance for us? This then leads
> manifestly to an impasse when it is projected onto the Chinese
> terrain. After having emphasized the functionality of the void (of
> the hub in the cart which allows the wheel to turn, of the hollow
> in the vase which allows it to contain, of the doors and windows
> in the room which allow it to be inhabited), the *Laozi* indeed con-
> cludes: 'At the level of the there is, it works as a benefit / at the
> level of the there is not, it works as functioning' (§ 11). Usually
> this is translated as 'Being offers possibilities / It is through

non-being that we utilise them' (translation by Liou Kia-hway
(Lao-tzeu, 1967); the analogous translation by François Houang
and Pierre Leyris is: 'Being has capabilities / Which non-being
employs' (Lao-tzeu, 2009)). Transposed into the language of
Being, the formula inevitably slips into contradiction (and then
leads, as the only possible way out, to a mystical reading which
the West, as it lightens what would be its very weighty logic
of non-contradiction, accepts all too readily). Nevertheless, we
understand it as soon as we realize that the negation brought into
play, inscribed in a logic of processes that is not at all ontological,
means that 'there is not [anything actualized]', such as the void
just evoked by the preceding images, and it is not an emptiness of
existence. The 'functioning' is still diffuse at the level of the void
which, by means of de-saturating, reactivates communication (at
the level of the undifferentiating – harmonizing Ground: *wu*) and
is manifested (is concretized) as a 'benefit' particular to the state
of each individuated 'there is'. As the *Arts of Painting* of ancient
China especially never tires of pointing out, the 'void' (or rather
the 'emptying out') of the 'there is not', which is left blank by the
line, is what 'fully' allows the 'there is' (of the representation) to
assume its full effect (see Jullien, 2003: ch. 6). In contrast, to have
believed in the *a-priori* universality of the notion of Being and
thought that a functional equivalence would be enough to ground
the cross-referencing, would render the formula unreadable.

The *invariant* assumes a pre-established universality that is vertical and
overarching and in which we can without difficulty see that it goes back
to a reassuring metaphysic of the thing itself, or of the core of being,
whose cultural variants would be the secondary qualities or different
costumes. As for the *equivalent*, it no longer projects anything more
than a transversal universality by locating in the two cultures a possible
cross-reference point by which they place themselves in perspective and
alignment. At the most appropriately adjustable point it joins together
their two banks by creating a bridge between them (see, for example,
Unesco International Conference, 2005[1] – this was a typical example
of good will, but it was ineffective at the theoretical level). For all that,
doesn't this representation of the bridge, which is so convenient (could
we even do without it?), also give way too quickly to a simplistic image,

that of two cultures found face to face (opposite each other) and already looking at one another? For the risk is not simply that the effect of the equivalence remains illusory, as soon as it is taken out of context, and that 'the resemblances of detail' would be 'misleading', as the Indianists tell us, 'if they are isolated from the heterogeneous wholes' (Biardeau, 1964: 20). More especially, the difficulty to be overcome between two cultures which have for so long been unaware of one another is not so much that of difference as of what I call *indifference*. Not that the divergence might be too great (because it is 'so far', etc.: the temptation of exoticism), but that there is not even a common measure (one which the universal would give rise to in a minimal way) to measure it with. There is no common frame, given in advance, in which to set the 'same' and the 'other' in play. These two cultures do not speak to one another and do not even *see each other*. When Raimundo Panikkar seeks an equivalence to human rights in the Indian *dharma*, it is above all upon this that he stumbles: that, from the point of view of the *dharma*, the (European) conception of human rights remains 'indifferent'. This does not mean that Indian thought proposes to criticize it, or has even the slightest idea of suspecting it, but that it has scarcely any interest in it.

The specialists in distant civilizations have often evoked this in the margins of their work, when they take the time to step back and review their 'profession'. No matter how valuable these sighs and asides are, for anyone who 'has lived for a long time in the heart of a civilization alien to our own', this work of penetration still remains 'slow and difficult'; how many 'errors of interpretation one has to make' before having the feeling that one is starting to understand, having to 'forget everything that had previously appeared self-evident' . . . (Biardeau, 1964: 17). Because the more we challenge simplistic connections, the more it appears perilous to think of 'passing through' by following *the same threads* (which universality would extend), from one end to the other (even if we had the prudence and skill of a tightrope walker). Such a continuity does not exist. An irreducible rupture subsists, in their 'bathing' or ambiance, between these separated parts. Deconstruction here and reconstruction elsewhere, *de-* and *re-*categorization, have thus proved inevitable. If we undertake to compare (as all translation necessarily implies), we will equally *de-*compare, at least through commentary, to allow a glimpse of this remainder of the incomparable that, by translating, we have concealed (see Jullien, 2007: chs. 9 and 10).

Ordinarily, nonetheless, unlike what we see among anthropologists, who have largely theorized their practice, Orientalists themselves have hardly ever reflected upon this condition of work, but have offered it in the form of remarks or confidences. This is why philosophy, until now, has taken little account of it. It felt it could be dispensed with. As an experience remaining implicit, born of an infinity of silent corrections and accommodations, pursued from one day to the next and forming a *habitus* (what I would call the *profession*), it has needed the patience of a whole life, a continuous and discreet assimilation, an infinity of small 'moves', to generate this connivance through which, among specialists, we understand each other without having to spell things out, in spite of strained translations. When they render the 'there is' / 'there is not' of the *Laozi* by the opposition of Being and non-being, they 'know well', with a knowledge they do not, however, seek to probe, that this translation is effected by default and is inadequate, or rather that it is only one angle and that hence it is necessary to understand 'something else'. Why would we still continue to put off treating this resistance as fleeting instead of hoping to find its advantage for thought rather than its pitfalls? For it will only be possible to consider the question of a universality of cultures seriously when we have not only tested this difficulty, but also made good use of the (unique) illumination it brings to the debate; indeed, without the test of such resistance, this would not exist.

3 Let's recapitulate, in fact, by coldly aligning these reasons. The *question* of the universal might have been posed as such (and even actually imposed: as constraining and imperious) in the European frame alone, or might at least have been privileged from various sides, as much by the invention of the concept as by the legal status of the citizen or the economy of God's plan. One might, on the other hand, have difficulty in locating notions (even if these would be major representations, such as 'Being', 'truth', 'time' and so on) which, across the disparity of cultures, may appear *from the outset* to be universal. In each case, for want of invariants, one might no longer even have been assured of finding equivalents which bridge one and the other, since the perspectives engendered by the

various cultures are not able to be detached all that easily from their languages to reveal a targetable point of cross-checking (which one might nevertheless doubt – but on what level to situate it?). Would all of these reasons we see piling up negatively against it in the process of crossing cultures (and which, I should say, have until now been of hardly any interest to philosophy) be enough to finish off the notion of the universal and henceforth to condemn its use? Would this be to turn it into no more than an old totalitarian dream of philosophy, that one will admit was a little delirious and which it is time to forget? On what might the universal otherwise still be founded? Or to put it the other way round: what do all of these relativizations, applied at the same time from within and outside of European culture, not bite into when we already see a universal breaking through which could not be put on trial?

For we see that all the demands of a cultural singularity, which make their voices heard with increasing strength the world over, will come up against this point. Once it appears, even if only in a single culture (the European, which has drawn its strength from it, or has at least been defined by it), the demand made by universality can no longer be relegated. Or, if there is effectively something *prima facie* liberatory and even joyful and jubilatory (that jubilation found in the earliest times) in conceiving oneself finally released from that presumed imperative [*devoir-être*] of the universal, not to recognize nonetheless that such a focal point is henceforth inscribed in the history of the world turns inevitably into denial. We can challenge this aspiration to universality, criticize it, denounce it, break with it, but its demands are not, for all that, reduced. The poorly assumed (on the part of Europe) presumption does not at all annul the need it has brought to recognition. Even if all representations of the universal will have collapsed in turn and become null and void, the *concept* of the universal itself is still there springing up. Indeed, the universal would be that signifying void whose successive replenishments, as soon as we cast a retrospective gaze on them, are revealed to this point as transitory and contingent, no longer leaving even an illusion about their hegemonic character; we nonetheless see that this void we reproach it for does not prevent it from operating. Or rather the contrary is true and it is from this that the universal draws its strength of resistance. It is this very *void*, which no signifier can fulfil or satisfy, which causes it still to operate.

Likewise, even if today we have ceased to call into question whether the universalism Europe has extolled might in fact only have been the universalization of its own culturalism; even if we actually see that, when Europe represented itself as the bearer of universal human interests in the period which led it to globalization, it was really only a matter of a new (and ultimate?) avatar of its theology of incarnation, we could still not be rid of what leaps out at us even more forcefully than a statement – which has a combat value: an operability of the universal remains, but it is precisely the opposite of what one might expect. It actually does not consist in a given positive, whatever it might be and as suspect as it is, of the order of values, but in this negative function: that, precisely, of *emptying out* every formation-institution of its certainty, born of the totalization which is sufficient to itself, and of reopening a breach in this comfort of the enclosure. The function of the universal, in other words, impossible to contain and always reborn, is to disturb any saturation-satisfaction – the one, precisely, which the Van Eyck brothers painted in their Ghent Altarpiece. In order to understand it, it is still necessary to change completely the basic representation upon which it is established. Where it is concerned, it is necessary to get rid of all lazy representations of a 'constitutive' or a 'given' (that of a universal implied in human nature, or of some 'common ground' of humanity in the name of which all people 'are alike' and so on), and to conceive of the universal in the opposite way as a strict agent and vector (and as such one that is inexhaustible) of *promotion*. This requires that it be treated as that principle which, divested of all acquired completeness and already surrounded with a fresh expectation, leads (but in an intrinsic, immanent way) beyond it.

> The very history of ideological struggles led against European universalism, especially as they have been seen to develop during these last decades in the USA and on the African continent, appear to me to have been very correctly analysed in this sense (especially around Ernesto Laclau, 1999: 131) – and they merit being taken as testimony. For, in distancing themselves from the universalist point of view the political left has traditionally borne, the movements demanding rights for cultural minorities (Black people under Apartheid, the Chicanos of the West coast of the US, homosexuals, all the excluded) have extolled a radical

particularism, and have no less had to realize that the only future their demands had was linked to the fact that they themselves did not respect them very much (as though it was simply a matter of a frame imposed on them in the negotiations), as they reclaimed and *revived* for themselves the exigency of universality. This is so even for the one which the dominant universalisms have abandoned by disregarding the legitimacy of their demands – that is to say by maintaining them in exclusion. The universal is therefore a weapon which turns on those who hold to it and it passes unremittingly from hand to hand. For it is finally the universal (and not particularism – since this is logically as one with them) which furnishes the only true denial of established universalisms. Or, put another way, isn't universalism a universal that has betrayed itself by being satisfied with itself and becoming dominant?

The fact that the demands of minority groups might still be made in the name of some universal principle, as is ordinarily recognized, should not therefore be conceived uniquely in terms of concession. It does not simply mean that all singularity is understood only by opposing a universalist pretension denounced as hegemonic, and that it remains, because of this, implicitly dependent upon it; nor that it would otherwise place itself in danger by having to admit in practice an equal legitimacy to any antagonistic or concurrent particularism. And one must therefore, of political necessity, introduce some mediation that is universalist in character, as an instance of regulation, to allow them to coexist. But what is more essentially at stake is that all differential identity which would realize itself completely loses consciousness of itself and annuls itself. The universal, however, is that *effect of lack* which reveals it to itself and creates its vocation. And so, never being filled up, it is led to transform itself, at the same time as it transforms its other, and therefore ceases to be satisfied with its own identity: not to enclose itself and stay within it, – otherwise at risk of also ending in a form of exclusion which, in its triumph, would be equally abusive – it would turn it over.

If I have referred to the experience of these struggles, it is because they finally reveal what philosophy has for a long time concealed, but of which the very difficulty of defining the universal in a homogenous way nevertheless allows a presentiment: that the universal is not a pure speculative object, and that its true nature and, as such, its legitimacy are revealed only in a situation of tension and by confrontation. Moreover, that it is always the tool of a struggle and a rending, whether this would be intellectual, social or political. The universal will not consequently be reduced to one thing or another. Nor will the universal be limited to a value as content (of an ideological nature), that of the various forms of universality which have succeeded one another in the course of History, invoked by way of values by the triumphant Europe-centrism migrating from one to the other, and which claim in turns to incarnate it. Obviously, such a plenitude and enclosure of the universal compromises it. Or, rather, the universal is conceived against them, against these universalisms which, it must be recognized, most often, never even dream of being surprised by what they exclude (for example, women or Black people excluded from civic society).

Nor is the universal limited to being a residue (of a logical nature), just remaining implicit, as a background, in the claim of the singular. For it would be unable to justify itself just by what (according to the ambiguity inherent in all opposition and which also renders it conservative) any (particularist) position still needs from its (universalist) opponent in order to affirm itself – in other words, by the fact that, through posing my singularity, at the same time I affirm the context from which I detach it (according to the familiar way that negation is dependent on the affirmation it denies). The legitimacy of the universal in relation to the singular, in other words, is not simply of the order of condition. Nor is it limited to non-contradiction, so that every individual would self-refute himself from the moment he abandoned it (thus the 'right to difference' is self-contradictory if it does not recognize itself as itself a universal right, and so on).

Neither purely residual, as the only ground of understanding of all particularisms, nor indulging in the fixed content of any universalism, the universal is therefore what is lacking completeness, or what is *continually defective*, which continually sends us back to that function, as I indicated earlier, of the *negative*. It is that force of appeal that is not content with any given, circumscribed as it is and however vast it might be, but from the interior of this given, turns it towards its overflowing. In other words, it is this emptying-out effect inscribing the imperious necessity for its renunciation at the heart of any limitation. Through it all totalization would be unable to accept and reassure itself as such, but it opens up again onto the unlimited or, more accurately, the illimitable. With it, the horizon once again slips away and does not settle on any contour that it has reached. This is why the universal is dynamic: in thought but also in History. It is the unconditioned in movement which, extending non-exclusion ever further, in this way works not only the field of theoretical elaborations, but also that of political configurations, maintaining under its pressure every form–structure–institution.

In the final analysis, the functional interest of the universal lies in the fact that it maintains a transcendence (an 'under transcendence', as we speak of being 'under pressure'), but one which remains internal (and does not take advantage of any 'Appeal'). In other words, it poses an absolute (as unconditioned or, more accurately, as unconditionable), which is not religious, or rather which now bestows the religious upon us. Thus, this is what especially draws the *common* after it and promotes it. Thanks to it, the *common* (of politics) does not sink into any estab-lished belonging, is not confined to any acquired sharing, but is led to extend itself, as we have seen when following the history of the City State, in the direction of an expansion knowing of no end. In this case, if it is simply the demand that the universal in itself continually activates, from where would the common find the idea of growing and progressing ever more? It is the universal that by its rigour, from logic to History, is impelled towards this 'universal community' (*civitas universa*) of categories, people and the Elect; and therefore it overturns the common of communitarianism. Thus, beyond all the instituted and satisfied universalisms, the universal retains an emancipatory and subversive ('insurrectionary', as Etienne Balibar (1997: 441), quite correctly calls it) character. We should therefore not be amazed that all of the trials of the former, as justified as they may be, would be unable to extinguish its vigour. For it does not mislead us: the universal represents an ideal because it keeps humanity in pursuit, and not because it would claim to have finally overcome the individual or the singular, the price of which we now recognize.

4 However, will this *ideal* status of the universal still be able to stand firm when confronted with the diversity of cultures? For, no longer even being sure of finding bridges, discernible among cultures, that would allow them to communicate transversally together, we are now driven to this questioning – a final position in which to entrench ourselves before the collapse. What is there that nonetheless links all cultures *a priori*, and on what plane should their encounter be assumed – since it is never to be completely assured by experience nor to be given metaphysically, contrariwise, by some 'human nature', in such a way as to be able to claim once more to be entitled to make them 'enter into dialogue'? The second question, the counterpart of the first, will be concerned with the subject: how can we still adhere to the values we want to pose as absolute (the strong gesture of political will), and therefore that *should be* universal, although we know perfectly well, now that Europe-centrism is no longer strong enough to hide it from us, that they find themselves ignored or even contested by other cultures? From this arises what creates a dilemma today. Do we necessarily have to tip over, brutally and without further ado, into a lazy relativism now that we can no longer be satisfied with the facile universalism which has for so long deluded Europe?

For want of a response to both questions, we will in fact abandon the question of the dialogue of cultures to what it so often is: to the ideological haziness which renders it so inconsistent but so much more voluble – a babbling of fine sentiments. Indeed, to advance the notion of the *ideal*, as I will start doing in order to confer an impregnability upon this cultural universal, will not in itself suffice. The end point is too compromised, corrupted as it is from within by philosophical idealism, for it to be possible for us to take cover in it without too much ambivalence. At least, if the notion is valid and if we want to hold on to it, its use is to be reinvested, to be constructed or, more accurately, to be *propped up*. It should be separated from the vague aspirations and the poignancy by which European culture ordinarily hopes to find an escape route (be it a nebulous one) in constructions judged too constraining for its reason.

We already see Kantian criticism opportunely lend support to this. In the *Critiques* of Pure Reason and Judgement (see Kant, 1978: §§ 8-9 and 18-22),[2] separate but converging angles are provided from which to approach these two questions less tentatively and once more to mobilize the ideal. Since Kantianism has most effectively pinpointed the question of the universal, it is proper, once again, to return to it. Kant both fixed the idea of an ethical universal as transparent, and subject from the outset only to the requirement of being validated by knowledge, and furnished the first outline for going beyond it (moreover, isn't the achievement of all great philosophy to bring coherences to a culmination and stabilize them, while at the same time already producing fresh engagements – the initial weapons – that will start to bring them into question?). For if I speak here of angles, of support, of propping up, it is because we know that Kant himself did not envisage these questions, had no idea of their significance, since he did not apply his gaze to other cultures (even had no idea that he should), and he developed his questions within the fold of the European tradition alone, that of a theory of the faculties. But he nevertheless defined its conditions of ideality which, however, breaking with inneism, can illuminate the two faces of what now appears, fundamentally, to be the same problem – on the one side, or the first facet of the question, by conceiving of a status of the idea as a representation of reason which might be in a position to elevate itself to the *unconditioned*, for want of effectively producing knowledge from it; on the other (the second facet of the question), according to the requirements of an *absolute judgement* concerning values and such that, although recognizing itself as singular, it nonetheless necessarily requires the adhesion of all, which is really the proclaimed characteristic of the universal.

> That an encounter between cultures might never actually be real-
> ized integrally (that one might never be able to detach completely
> from what is privileged in a culture by way of values and rep-
> resentations), but that such an encounter might not be 'illusory'
> either (that it might not be a pious wish to work patiently to
> produce, question after question, the conditions of such a possibil-
> ity), such is really, in fact, to respond to the first point, the ideal
> status of a *universal* that would no longer be speculative in relation
> to the theory of knowledge but *cultural*. This is an ideal then that
> signifies, by transposition, precisely this: that if, in experience,
> there are no values and representations which allow us to emerge
> entirely from the conditioning appropriate to various cultures,
> singular as they are in their implicit choices (notably due to the

fact, as we are well aware, that there is no more a back-language than there is a back-world to which to gain access), this does not for all that annul the validity of a universal of cultures as a notion of something 'unconditioned' or *transcending* all the given conditions for forming an aspiration to this surpassing. Through them, this 'under what conditions', as Kant said of the ideas of reason, the values and representations of all the cultures of the world allow themselves *a priori* to be subsumed (the proof of which is that one can speak from the outset of 'culture' in respect of them), will assume in this way a definite theoretical status, even if it never really happens, no matter what the degree of dialogue between cultures, so that the values and representations might be able to emerge integrally from their own conditioning and affirm value, without the abuse of imperialism, in a way which would be absolutely universal.

We have to take account of both at the same time. On the one hand, as soon as we enter into the denseness of languages, social and mental systems, customs and ages, and eliminate facile misunderstandings, we measure (as I have only just started to do here), the extent to which all cultures are still folded into perspectives which are inherent to them and continue to be so even when they become uniform, as today's globalized culture thoroughly does through a constant chain of influence. Can we not in fact see that today's world culture, notwithstanding that soon there may be no difference relative to itself for it to encounter – indeed, it might think it has integrated everything on the planet – nonetheless cannot claim universality as long as it also remains so folded within the pre-suppositions which condition it and render it equally singular? It just has less awareness of it, and because it extends its uniform domain without encountering further resistance, does not even suspect what is particular in it. On the other hand, the *idea* of universal understanding between cultures, present or past, a horizon never reached or even attainable since it is always hiding behind all the proposed universalisms, plays a no lesser *regulatory* role in guiding the search for it (Kant, 1969). It gives this search its urgency and even imposes it upon the mind as a necessary task to be pursued 'as far as it is possible', even if its conclusion is never seen; at the same time it continually leads the mind into this work.

It is this idea, and under this rubric, that of the unconditioned or the 'transcendental', which is alone able to assure its condition of possibility in the dialogue of cultures, so offering a way out of its difficulties.

5 It will be necessary to do still more violence to Kant in order to drive him onto the second terrain, to the flip-side of the question: to transpose what he tells us about the judgement of the beautiful to the cultural judgement of values. To do violence to him, in fact, since, for him, the good, as it is given by practical reason, is determined by a conception which renders it objectively universal, independently therefore of all cultural conditioning. It was necessary to wait until Nietzsche for the idea of a *perspective* on values to be brought to light, to be put in its proper place. And yet, does thinking of articulating together the universal and the singular – the absolute and the conditioned – by taking account of the diversity of cultures and in the very operation of the judgement – cause morality to deviate from its autonomy? Let us recall the Kantian deduction about the beautiful: when I consider something 'beautiful' it is really a question of a singular judgement, even as I claim that all people necessarily agree with it – I do not allow anyone, in other words, to have another opinion. I make it into a rule for everyone, or at least I assign it to everyone, as though this was a matter of an objective judgement (and this is different from the judgement made about the 'agreeable', which I willingly recognize as something to which I alone am committed). Without therefore having to verify it by any evidence, indeed even if I state that it is widely disapproved of by people around me, I no less claim *a priori* a universal approval for this judgement. And it is legitimate for this very reason.

Or at least this would be the first way of representing things, a useful angle for emerging from the impasse. To make it easier to overcome these initial perils, the Scylla and Charybdis of the intercultural, which I have designated on one side as *facile universalism* (naively projecting its vision of the world onto the rest of the world) and, on the other side, as *lazy relativism* (condemning cultures to imprisonment in an identity with specific values). But for all that, when I have no aesthetic of morality in view, what can justify me referring to the judgement of the beautiful, rather than the good, in order to found a universality of judgements with a bearing on values? The answer is precisely that we currently have an obligation to integrate the absolute into the singular perspective appropriate to diverse cultures, since now we are no longer able to understand ourselves other than as *cultural subjects* (thereby making the 'transcendental subject' at least partially bankrupt). Thus the step I make Kant take at this point is somewhat forced but, as a step sideways, it still gives an indication of a way out – it furnishes something like a tangent by which to emerge from the aporia. Thus, don't Europeans, when they demand human rights for all peoples, match them with their own ideal, as is done in respect of the beautiful: a provisional, non-conditional, validity which they consider ought to be universal, without for all that possessing a transcultural concept of such a value? If they do so in a legitimate way, then such a judgement is obviously still not completely detachable from a certain conditioning by their representations (a subject to which I will return), notably from their inveterate dependency (to what extent is this resolvable?) upon the theological, from their straining for abstraction in the face of any relation of dependency, from their historical struggles for emancipation and so on.

Didn't Kant then give a signal precisely towards the only possible place (that of ideality) from which such legitimacy could originate? Or rather he illuminated at one and the same time the fact that such legitimacy might be undeniable but might not for all that be able to designate the site, or the theoretical seat, from which it draws this authority. And one could even say, in a more radical way, the fact that such a judgement (like that which pronounces the absolute value of human rights) either reveals an unchallengeable exigency that could nevertheless not be named, or illustrates a necessity of which it would be unable to give an account, is what properly characterizes it. In this way, in effect, Kant tells us, 'it can only be called exemplary' (*exemplarisch*). In other words: 'it is a necessity of the assent of *all* to a judgement regarded as exemplifying a universal rule which cannot be formulated' (*ein Beispiel einer allgemeinen Regel, die man nicht augeben kann*) (1978: 67, 'Analytic of the beautiful', § 18). This rule, which is *universal*, but one *which cannot be shown*, is precisely the concept of the paradoxical exigency and sets to work in an undetermined way (therefore having a 'regulatory' function) in accordance with which cultures the world over today constantly dialogue when they strive to agree upon their values while trying to emerge from their perspectivism. Let's return to the preceding case and so progress step by step along this litigious road: if it is no longer possible for anyone to deny that the ideal of human rights is the product of a singular and conditioned cultural history, they will still no less be considered to be *exemplary* of what is Unconditioned.

That they refract a source of illumination on their particular plane (of the human), whose origin they cannot designate, does not, for all that, make these human rights an idealist construction. For if this lack of determinacy legitimately belongs to the ideal, as it is unconditioned, the subjective principle which justifies the universal validity that such a judgement requires can nevertheless be revealed by following Kant, and it does so by returning precisely to the common. Isn't it a 'common sense' (*Gemeinsinn*) which is definitively to be invoked, in the way that Kant does here in respect of the beautiful, as the sole remaining condition of possibility for the communication demanded between cultures? It is under this supposition alone, in fact, that the culturally subjective necessity of judgement is represented as objective in allowing that what I personally experience applies *at the same time* to everyone. 'Common sense', which then ceases to be of the understanding (that of the currently accepted meaning, when the most widely shared principles are no more than obscurely represented in it), nor is it any longer a merely aesthetic common sense (grounding the communicability of the judgement of the beautiful in an *a-priori* way) – I will call it precisely the *common sense of the human*. This is where cultures are ultimately able to meet, only on this *a-priori* side of languages as well as of conceptions, where there is no longer any need for mediation, just as, in the final resort, the transculturality of a judgement is authorized by it, even if it is unable to find its concept within it.

We still need to see what a 'community of meaning' might signify when it is joined to the 'human'. For this does not mean tipping back again into the metaphysical naiveties of the 'ground', or base, in which thought takes refuge by means of a simplistic imagination, contenting itself with papering over the cracks, when it fails to think about the foundation (the well-known 'common ground' of humanity invoked so widely in the dialogue of cultures), since this common sense is really what shows through vividly in all experience, just as it continually speaks to us in every language. Nor does it mean making a sacrifice to the purely reactive and sensible conception to which, despairing of the constructions of reason, morality has been able to give way (this meaning of the human then going back to 'pity', something which would be found at the origin of all morality throughout the world; cf. what Schopenhauer, the first comparativist philosopher, says on the subject), since an intelligence which consequently makes itself clear in rational judgements as well as in representations that conceive of values no less develops from it and through it. Nor is it any longer a question simply of the single fold to be found within a theoretically failing position to give a minimal notional consistency to what is too thinly spread to remain analysable (common sense then becoming the platitude of 'good sense'). But I believe it is the only applicable plane upon which the two, experience and the *a priori*, the common of sharing and the imperative [*devoir-être*] of the universal (since the only thing we can be sure of, independently of all experience, is that it is universally shared by all experience) may be linked. It is therefore within it, within this *common sense of the human*, that cultures originally understood each other and that enables them to move beyond their idioms so as to open themselves up to what Kant so aptly named a universal 'communicability' or 'shareability', *allgemeine Mitteilbarkeit* – the thought of it will be taken further to track the various ways in which the common is crushed.

X On human rights – the notion of universalizing

1 Human rights provide the perfect example of what, from the judge-ment of the beautiful, or more precisely of its paradoxical (but legiti-mate) articulation of the absolute and the singular, is transposable to the order of values and politics. Westerners pose them, and even impose them, as having to be universal, although it is obvious that these rights came from a particular historical conditioning; they claim that all peoples subscribe to them absolutely, without possible exception or reduction, although they cannot fail to state at the same time that over the world other cultural options are unaware of them or contest them.[1] For to what extent can Europe take this denial, that of the forced and even hazardous composite ordering, of which these rights are the product at the very heart of its own history? At best all that this will verify is what we have already perceived of the motley, not to say chaotic, nature of how the universal was fabricated: the Declaration of the Rights of Man in 1789, for example, was born from multiple preparatory and even, in part, incompatible projects, and, in the course of its drafting, became the object of an infinity of negotiations and compromises. It was formed from the association of fragments taken from various sides – one term here, a sentence there, its articles corrected, carved up and re-written (see Fauré, 1988: 15, as well as Gauchet, 1989). It was recognized, and voted upon, by the authors themselves, as 'unfinished'. One of them confided on the evening of its adoption that 'No doubt the worst of all the drafts is perhaps the one adopted' (Adrien Duquesnoy, representa-tive of Bar-le-Duc, quoted in Fauré, 1988: 16). But, *at the same time*, just as any reference to actual events was prudently kept at a distance, just as everything that appeared too specific was avoided, through fear of increasing the disagreements, this text, written in haste and against a backdrop of hesitation, in which bad faith also mingled at times with enthusiasm, assumes the form of an abstraction which gives it a sacred quality. Presenting itself as unbegotten, born fully armed from the brain of the constituents, it is adorned with a mythic aura (as if 'in the presence

of and under the auspices of the Supreme Being') and it makes a claim to a pre-established universality.

Wouldn't it once again be the case that, contrary to what it says about itself, the pretension to universality is the only way a threatening hetero-geneity can be held together – that is, by leaving it behind? It orders the present dispersion like a perspective line and projects its reconciliation into an abstract beyond; or, as is currently the case in European ideology, it is the sublimation that offers a way out of the violence of contradictions (through repression – promotion). For throwing people off the scent in this way (towards its supposed universality) is not without effect either: an enthusiasm and a drive well up within it. The difficulties in the pro-duction of the text being hidden, it then appears striking in its historical success; every trace of its contingency is effaced and it becomes (and in a legitimate way) drawn towards what is ideal and necessary. And it does this to such an extent that this Declaration of 1789 has established a lineage (which would be taken up again in 1793, 1795, 1848, 1946, 1948, 1950 . . .). Nostalgia can then be expressed, at the time of the drafting of the Declaration of 1946, for the brevity – majesty – simplicity of 'our great text of 1789', while we are 'aware that the articles in the text of 1946 have various origins and have been thought about in several languages, and been translated from some languages into others' (Georges Vedel, quoted in Fauré, 1988: 17), and so on. The contemporary acknowledge-ment of its composite nature is repeated, and again forgotten along with its subsequent smoothing over by History. That such a Declaration might so constantly be re-written shows sufficiently well that the universality to which it makes a claim is not a *given*, but should be seen as a regulating idea, in the Kantian sense: an idea that is never satisfied and which guides the research indefinitely, one which is set to work.

> It would moreover be difficult to hide the original *conditioning* of
> the Declaration of 1789 under the unconditional universality of
> its formulations: that it was born from a protest against an already
> damaged royal arbitrariness; that it was understood principally as
> a reaction against the privileges of a nobility, hastening its decline;
> or that religious freedom was defended in it due to the vigilance of
> the Protestants; or that, under the general question of 'property'
> (in the plural or the singular? – see article XVII), the question of

the redemption of feudal rights was thrashed out, and so on. That is why it had to be taken back to the drawing board and redrafted. This would occur after only a few years, in other words at each fresh inflexion of the Revolution: the re-drafting of 1793 bringing to the surface the social question and especially that of work; that of 1795 in reaction to revolutionary violence by insisting on 'duties' as much as, responding to the danger of factions, on the 'universality' of citizens, and so on. Slower to appear (even now are we fully aware of it?), but just as undeniable, are the ideological options which have marked it (and these will become really prominent only with the divergence of cultures) – whether this might be the idea of a social contract or an 'associative pact', or of 'happiness' put forward as an ultimate aim, or of the conception of humanity based solely on the relation between an 'individual' born 'free' and the sovereignty of the Nation and its Law, and, above all, the unproblematic character of the continuity instigated between the state of nature ('Men born . . .') and civil society ('. . . and remaining free and equal in law'). Finally, if this Declaration is sacralized, it is really because religious investment, withdrawing from revealed religion (and from that moment becoming insignificant), has nowhere else to go, in the course of the process of secularization marking Europe, than to make Man absolute in his 'Rights'.

But when it comes to 'rights', why would they be precisely those of Man, who alone is able to make himself absolute by rising to the unconditioned status of a universal? We need to remember what specialists in Roman law have learned in this respect when they show us that, far from being the legitimate fruit of the ideas of right as the Latins conceived it, human rights represented more of a twisting of it (see in particular Villey, 1986). They were born from a relatively strange conjunction on the threshold of the modern age, in which many diverse influences were entangled. Moreover, this was the case for the nominalism inherited from the late medieval thinkers (Duns Scotus, William of Ockham), which retained from substantial reality only that of the individual alone, and for the second strand, which was scholastic (and Spanish, Suárez especially), inventing as it did a theology that was no longer ascendant but deductive, and which separated *natura pura*, the pure nature of man as God originally created it and on which philosophy can be content to work, from a 'super-

nature' to which Revelation alone gives access. It is from this generic definition of mankind, from the principles of Reason inscribed in his nature
and forming the natural law, that the science of law will from then on be
drawn, which is why it can be conveniently absolutized as 'universal'.

> Previously many jurists (in Rome), we are taught, had conceived
> of the law as essentially being exercised within the boundaries
> of a city, as *jus civile*, implying in this capacity judge, procedure
> and institutions, and taking the stage only if there was a dispute
> (*causa*) acting as an object limiting the scope of the controversy,
> and the law was confined to the definition of Justice aiming to
> establish the appropriate apportionment (the *aequum*) in the way
> goods and charges were shared. It was conceived essentially as
> a *relation* to determine, which formulations and codifications
> never completely coincided with. In this way the law, even in
> its most general conceptions and rules, far from being a product
> of pure reason, the projection of an egalitarian ideal engendered
> by our minds, became first of all the object of an enquiry which
> developed principally from the observation of relations between
> beings. It essentially aimed to attribute to each person what was
> due to them depending on the position they held.

It will therefore be necessary to reflect upon what our promotion of
human rights, which are declared to be universal, possesses, in Europe
itself, that is historical and consequently singular – and, above all, to
recall those sudden conjunctions and mutations in the history of ideas
if we do not want to continue to be mistaken about the universality that
can be imparted to them. There is no point in going back from various
directions to trace their genesis, since the way they were hatched had the
explosive character of an event that was at once logically deductible and
invented. As we are in fact aware, everything changed when Hobbes put
forward the notion of a right of nature (*jus naturale*) as no longer being
constituted from multiple juridical relations linking all beings together,
but which became *freedom* as a natural and unique right, freedom as what
each person possesses 'to use his own power as he will himself for the
preservation of his own Nature' (Hobbes, 1997: 189). An enthusiast of
Euclid, Hobbes thereby deduced human rights from a basic definition
and in his approach applied the method of analysis from simple elements,

then by a re-composition through synthesis, learned from Galileo. Keen on theology (even if he was a materialist), he borrowed from its vocabulary the notion of a 'state of nature' which he conceived by secularizing it as a scattering of individuals from whom society is abstractly reconstructed. It is a thought that is therefore eminently singular, and which was even born out of a particularly tense ideological conjunction, which no doubt gives it its strength, making this conception at once contemporary with the arrival of the subject in classical philosophy as well as being carried along by the relation which was then established between the State and the Individual. From this comes the idea of a right which itself becomes the pure emanation of such a subject – it is a 'subjective' right, which means that it is also one that is absolute and unlimited, as the freedom to act 'according to one's own judgement' and unshackled by any law. 'Human rights' were born.

> What followed, as we know, were no more than improvements, if I dare express it in this way: either this liberty might be globally sacrificed to a sovereign power within the frame of a social contract so as to put an end to the endemic war born of rivalry resulting from covetousness (in Hobbes himself), or it would be redistributed and diffracted into plural liberties, through the notions of work and property, and so no longer allow a rupture to be marked out between the state of nature and society (in Locke). From that point on there has remained that major option which has continuously, in spite of its original mark and particularity, sought to impose itself as a universal imperative [*devoir-être*], that of Man as an individual endowed with total freedom, one therefore equal and from the start to be shielded from any hierarchy, but whom society always threatens to enslave (Rousseau).

2 Imposed only in the modern era – even if we can follow what formed their bedrock from the time of the Greeks, through various contributions, in multiple castings, especially that inexhaustible one of Stoic morality infiltrating Christianity – human rights are of course the product of a double (Western) abstraction – that both of 'rights' and of the 'human'. Of *rights*: from the reciprocity of the relation, the notion of rights isolates the side of the subject by privileging the defensive angle of the demand and emancipation (of the non-alienation) devoted to the

source of freedom ('duty' in this respect is itself only a (compensating) guarantor which participates equally from this optic). Of *man*: that which is isolated from all vital context, from the animal to the cosmic, the social and political dimension itself arising from a later construction. It is only as an individual that 'Man' is absolutized, since no aim is conceived for any association except to 'preserve' his 'natural and imprescriptible rights' (see the Declaration of 1789, article 2). Isolation, abstraction and absolutization, going hand in hand, have therefore been the price to be paid for this universal to be erected. What then is *at the same time* unravelled under these conjoined operations? Nothing less than what could be called, symmetrically, the *integration* of the human in its world – an 'integration' precisely signalling towards the opposite of what is expressed as *alienation*. Such a loss can already be identified in Europe's own modern history.

> Significantly even the *family*, a minimal level of integration introducing its mediation between the individual and society, is absent from the Declarations of 1789 and 1793 (and will appear only in 1795 in a way amazingly recalling the Confucian 'five relations' – could there have been an influence?: 'No one is a good citizen unless they are a good child, a good father, a good brother, a good friend, a good spouse'). In the 1948 Declaration, the reference to 'all the members of the human family' still has a vaguely metaphorical and allusive status that is more rhetorical than explanatory; in any case it is not well founded. Thus, in ridding it of any religious dimension (the Supreme Being of 1789 is invoked only as a witness), by unravelling the group (caste, class, *gens*, tribe, kinship, guild, corporation and so on), refusing any pre-established forms of hierarchy (since equality is posed in it as a basic principle), and above all by cutting man off from 'nature' (concern for the environment and its lasting development returning only very recently, as though a sense of urgency had become necessary today for us to make up for what we had ill-advisedly neglected), the concept of human rights selects and *assumes the side* of the human. The options it inscribes within it cannot themselves advance any justification, at least ultimately, other than that of their universality. What follows is the logical circle in which the thought of the universal appears enclosed. It is

not only the end but also the guarantor and the security of its own operation of abstraction.

I will propose generalizing these two cultural logics which come face to face with each other – that is, of *emancipation* (through the universality of human rights) or of *integration* (in the midst of affiliation: familial-corporate-ethnic-cosmic). The question will henceforth, for the world to come, be to know whether they will continue to be irreconcilable. So let us one final time renew our survey into the elsewhere of cultures. If we consider Indian culture in relation to the European, these logics will appear effectively exclusive at the same time as the overall coherences, manifesting this character of 'option', in fact they become a lot more readable on both sides. Or else, if the concept of human rights finds no echo in the thought of classical India (or, expressed in the opposite way, if the latter is revealed as somewhat indifferent to it), it is really because there is within it an encounter of inverse commitments, but ones that are *equally intelligible*.

> Even from afar we are aware – as a solid fact before which European intelligence, as soon as it pays attention to the fact, is seized with an irrepressible vacillation – that in India there is no *isolation* of 'Man'. Not in relation to animals: the cutting off of people from them is only pertinent in an inadequate way once the re-births of one into the other is admitted. Moreover, the animal equally possesses the power to infer and to know (if animals are incapable of giving themselves any other aim than the immediate, it is not by virtue of a congenital incapacity, but rather because they have no access to the Veda – something they share with the lower castes). Nor in relation to the world: as the human psyche is only an ensemble of organs destined passively to transmit external givens, so human interiority, which is destined only to react to what the world supplies it with, is not in a position to take a genuine step back in relation to it. Adherence to the world is such that it is not conceived as a natural order from which humanity can be detached. Nor finally in relation to the group, which, determined hierarchically through its religious function, is the primary reality in which the individual finds himself with only a minimal status, one which, being irreducible, is confined to the psycho-physiological of that which suffers or feels pleasure.

This means that European philosophy, since Schopenhauer, has to be undermined. 'Man', in India, is so little an entity that his life and death are devoid of all significance, destined as they are to repeat themselves indefinitely. In any case, the individual is not in himself endowed with a proper power of initiative and creation. If he is then really a 'himself' (*atman*), correlated with the absolute, to whom deliverance is accessible, there is still nothing within him that changes if he is condemned to be re-born at the lowest level of beings: what therefore does he have that is specifically human? Indeed, when man separates from his group and turns himself into a 'renouncer', an individual act *par excellence*, this is not in order to recognize his individuality, but on the contrary to abolish it.

> If *dharma* is the term that is most obviously impossible to translate into European languages, to the point that no possible equivalent for it can be recognized (it can be translated equally well as an element – quality – origin – norm of conduct – character of things – morality – right – truth – justice and so on), it is because it is clearly understood, in what it thereby succeeds in bending together, only from the point of view of that which assures the *cohesion* of things: it maintains them together, in a co-herent (and non-aberrant) way, and allows their continuity. So let us dare to draw the consequences from this if, as I earlier indicated, it is through thinking the *dharma* that an encounter may be entertained in relation to human rights posed as universal (see Raimundo Panniker, 1999). In fact, from that point on, what is at issue through the *dharma* is the totality of the sequence of beings, and the order it designates is recognized as necessary for the maintenance of the harmonious existence of the whole constituted by the 'Three worlds', and the individual can expect the worst calamities if he does not observe it. Is it then surprising that, under its aegis, there has been only a slight interest in highlighting 'human rights' limited to the very restrained, at the same time as constructed, framework of politics? This is all the more so in as much as it cannot be forgotten that the most elevated vocation is to absorb oneself into the undifferentiated Whole, a state in which the notion of a cosmic order (*dharma*) is itself shown to lose meaning. On the other hand, the hierarchical vision of Indian society also immediately implies that the *dharma* cannot have an

identical content for each group or caste of society. What the notion enjoins is rather that of having to find one's place in this global environment, thereby participating in the great metabolic function of the universe. We therefore find in India neither a principle of individual autonomy nor any idea of political self-constitution from which human rights might be declared. While Freedom is the last word of European thought, the Far East, when confronting it, inscribes 'harmony' – and, in this respect, India effectively corresponds with China (which has itself, moreover borrowed, the very notion of *dharma* – *fa* – through Buddhism). No doubt it is therefore rather the 'West' which, by introducing rupture as a source of forced entry and, consequently, of emancipation (already the *chôrismos* of the Greeks), constitutes a scandalous exception.

In fact it appears that, in the typology of cultures, human rights find themselves caught in the crossfire between two opposing sides. Their margin for flowering is tiny in spite of their universal pretension. When the perspective of transcendence dominates to the point of resulting in the constitution of another world, they are absorbed into an order, whether cosmic or theological, which goes beyond them, but when immanence prevails, they are not in a position to detach themselves from the spontaneous course of things and are unable to emerge from the power relations. Islam, of course, is in the first category. By totalizing the Revelation, the Koran and the Tradition emanating from it (*sunna*, *charia*, *fatwa* . . .) fix a law that, being of divine creation, 'attains, it is concluded, the final summit in the regulation of human relations' (Abu-Salieh, 1994: 14). Likewise, if it is claimed, through concession or to authorize a precedence, that human rights also find themselves implicated in it, this means in fact that they have no place (or reason) properly to constitute themselves. The fear of the Last Judgement, a first element of Islamic faith, not recognizing them on the autonomous level on which they are deployed, reduces them to insignificance.

China is in the second category. For how are 'human rights' expressed in Chinese, when being translated from the Western idea? *Ren* ('man')-*quan*. Properly designating balance and the operation of weighing up, *quan* serves equally to express both 'power', especially political power (*quan-li*), and what we understand by 'circumstance' or expedient (*quan-bian, quan-mou*). What this does, in its variation and the fact that it is opposed to the fixity of rules (*jing*), is to prevent the situation being blocked, but to continue to evolve in conformity with the logic of the process engaged upon. Likewise, the fact that these two meanings join at the heart of the same term and would both be conceived from the inflecting of balance makes us think that there is no determination of the real, at least in the final instance, except in the way the situation leans *of itself* to one or the other side. It is through 'circumstance' that the real continues to be modified so it may continue to be deployed (the notion of *bian-tong*), and the weight of 'power' is itself merely the result of such an inflection. That this might then be the term which serves to translate 'right(s)', when 'human rights' are at issue, demonstrates the extent to which it has to be twisted – even if this foreign graft has taken well in modern China and if we take account of the *community of intelligibility* which links up what is human (which I will develop later). And I will even insist on this point: when the young Chinese of Tiananmen Square demanded human rights they knew from that moment on what they were talking about as much as Westerners do. But the fact remains that the preceding divergence of thought cannot be ignored; if it is, there would be the danger of giving up the clairvoyance of all political engagement to. For if *right* has equally to take account of the differences in particular cases, it does not in itself emanate from the situation, in contrast *to power*, but transcends it through its ideality. In this respect it is undeniably a theoretical production that Europe has favoured.

Such is the *thin in-between quality* of human rights, to which their condition of cultural possibility is owed: they detach themselves (neither 'declaring' nor 'proclaiming' themselves) only by isolation and by a shift in categories. But the transcendence which belongs to them must not for all that be integrated into a superior order. Because if it were then a type of infraction would be absorbed into it, as happens in any theological culture. As far as the thought of immanence is concerned, for its part the response will still be to raise once more the old Taoist argument that the emergence of human rights and their demands is simply due to the loss of primitive Harmony: one would not dream of demanding them unless there has been a rupture in spontaneous understanding.[2] And so human rights are really the rupture of a plenitude. The universal which inhabits them, and without which they do not exist, must therefore be understood in a sense that is the opposite of any totalization – satisfaction – by which I see that we return once again to the inherent negativity of the universal.

3 To consider this trial initiated against human rights on the cultural scale impels us into a progressive inquisition of the universal, to which there is currently no end in sight. And, above all: (1) through its abstraction, the Declaration expounding them in this universal mode evades the unresolved contradictions of the historical situation which saw them appear: it is enough in this respect to raise ever so slightly the veil covering the genesis of successively re-written texts. On the other hand: (2) these human rights rest on pre-suppositions that were perhaps too hastily accepted – in the first place, that they could be founded on 'human nature', which is itself universal, the concept of which would be transcultural and transhistorical; that this might, moreover, be knowable, without the aid of any intuition or privileged Revelation, but simply through the organ of Reason; that it might, consequently, be radically cut off from any other reality, including that of the animal. Hence: (3), in spite of their proclaimed pretension, human rights arise from a particular ideology which they conceal or, even worse, are completely unaware of: retraction from the cosmos, loss of harmony, abstraction of the individual and determination of an irreducible status as *imago dei*, the primacy of the demand over the communitarian, and so on. Finally: (4), if human rights have benefited from a sacralization that has made them absolute, it is through the contemporary loss of the sacred divine and by transferring transcendence to them. Moreover, can we forget that they have been contested from two directions at the very heart of European thought? This is both in relation to their theological aspects (they can find an absolute foundation only by being integrated with Revelation) and from the Marxist perspective: 'human rights' are class rights, *Klassenrechte* (Marx, 1975: I, 229). It will be argued that evidence for this is given in the way in which they have historically so often been invoked to hide oppression and make it acceptable, and so on.

This is why so many disordered, but relatively concurrent, efforts are today made to save the universality of human rights – an ideological free-for-all, the source of a literature that is, it is true, inexhaustible:[3] everyone seeks a way out as they try to sidestep it by means of the radical nature of their conception. A picture can even be painted of these multiple contradictions. For no sooner is naive triumphalism at an end than the universal henceforth wants to be modest. It is actually by making itself minimalist that it hopes to survive the critiques put forward. But in doing so, is it following the right track?

(1) One might propose to *relativize* our conception of human rights so as to take cultural disparity into account (the theory of 'weak cultural relativism' concluding with the 'relative universality of human rights'),[4] whether by accepting they could be adapted to other cultures, or by leaving other cultures the latitude to develop their own 'equivalents'. But I have already said that human rights cease to exist if they are not posed as absolute: their imperative [*devoir-être*] being a principle, *a priori*, they can tolerate no contradiction.

(2) One might propose to *reintegrate* them into a more global and consensual thought of harmony (a discourse most frequent in the Far East). But I have already shown that their logic of emancipation through a breaking of the rules not only diverges from the *integration* whose principle is the thought of harmony, but even enters into overt conflict with it.

(3) One might propose to *find small elements of them*, in one form or another, *mutatis mutandis*, everywhere in the world. This time in the name of a *de facto* anthropological universality, we are led to a simple generality: thereby it is thought to locate them in the way reciprocal duties link the members of the community in China, or in the preservation of life in India and so on. But, at risk of losing all rigour, the notion of human rights cannot accept being diluted into notions with undefined contours, such as those of dignity or human values, open to various interpretations and above all uncontrollable in practice, to which they are then again led (all the more so in that this anthropological identification is always made solely in the language, or at least solely with the concepts, of Europe).

(4) One might propose to *reduce* their clear-cut qualities by downgrading the theoretical as well as the operative status of their

concept: they will be judged as more tolerable if they are seen only as a 'symbol'. But it is precisely by not blurring the clearness of their division into a nebulous halo, as well as by not loading them with a greater residual emotionality, that they will be rendered culturally transmittable (or rather it is the opposite).

(5) One might finally propose to *contract* their ambition on one point to render them indisputable – a bastion easier to defend. Human rights will be supported, for example, by invoking the intolerable character of child labour: isn't the right to education a primary, basic right (one on which all others depend) and, as such, one that cannot be denied? The fact remains that even notions of 'work' (as opposed to study, leisure or holidays) as well as those of 'childhood' (the entrance into the age of 'adult' activity varies widely according to civilizations) are, as we know, a long way from being directly transposable from one culture to another. This is shown by what the anthropologists teach us about 'primitive' peoples: what appears to us today to be alienation may not be for them as long as relations of exploitation have not become prominent. For it is contemporary ways of living, exported from the West, which imposed the idea that work and childhood *should be thought about as separate* and so child labour was conjured up as a glaring injustice in the name of an individual autonomy to which study alone gives access.

Will the claim of a universality of human rights in fact be satisfied just by those evolutions established in History, even if we grasp the necessity which has led to them in an undeniable way? To express this more specifically: does the universal legitimacy of human rights arise only from the fact that the Western way of life, born from the simultaneous development of science and capitalism, has in the end been imposed on the rest of the world, making it therefore necessary (or inevitable) from that moment on to adopt the ideology, at once social and political, of human relations which accompany these transformations? But we already know how much the universal is distinguished from the uniform, or rather that it is the inverse of it; and, on the other hand, we would be unable to hide from ourselves the fact that such an argument is fundamentally no more than opportunistic. Or would this legitimacy come from the fact that the European thought which brought human rights with it in fact expresses a historical progress, and because they constitute a benefit for humanity which, as such – following the example set by the development of science from the beginning of the seventeenth century and being contemporary with it – could itself only have been produced in Europe? Aside from the fact that this justification represents at least a tacit accusation of all other cultures, its critique seems self-evident, containing within it the most obtuse ethnocentrism: for in the name of what would such progress be judged if it is not *already* at the heart of a particular ideological frame (preferring autonomy to harmony, for example)?

These objections are enough to show that any *ideological justification* for a universality of human rights is a blind alley, just as any of the reductionist operations that have been proposed are meaningless: the claim to the universality of human rights in fact seems defensible to me only from a *logical* point of view. Rather than dreaming about blunting the concept of human rights by consigning it to accommodations that make them transculturally acceptable because they are given at a discount, I would myself reject this powerless but all the more voluble discourse of good will. I would take the opposite option: that of consolidating their conceptual effect, from which they benefit at once in *operativity* and *radicality*.

For, on the one hand, it is actually the abstraction by which they proceed which alone, by detaching them from their original culture and surroundings, renders human rights communicable to other cultures. In other words, it is not simply because the West promoted them at the moment it ascended to the summit of its power and could claim, through imperialism, to impose them on the rest of the world, that this is today discussed between nations, but also because this status of abstraction renders them isolatable and therefore intellectually manageable, conveniently identifiable and transferable. It follows that they become a privileged object (tool) for dialogue (one could not, for example, make 'harmony' a comparable stake because it is internationally disputable between cultures). On the other hand, what I understand by their capacity for conceptual radicality (or nudity) is that they grasp the human in its most elementary state, at the level of existence, envisaging man under this final condition, upstream from all others, which is therefore worth something unconditional: simply in so far as he *is born*. From this perspective, it is not then so much the individual (as an ideological

construction which still contains much that is arbitrary, as can easily
be shown) which is the target, as the fact simply that it is a question of
the human – 'of the human' here being less a possessive genitive (in the
sense of: what belongs to man) than a partitive: as soon as the human is
involved, an imprescriptible imperative [*devoir-être*] appears *a priori*.

However, as far as the logical structure of this notion that forms an
operative concept is concerned, I cannot leave matters there. The universalizing capacity of 'human rights' stems even more from this other fact:
that their *negative impact* (from the point of view of that *against which*
they are raised up) is infinitely broader than their *positive extension* (from
the point of view of that *to which* they adhere). There is a dissymmetry, in
other words, between the two faces of the notion. For if, from the point of
view of their positive content, we now know sufficiently well the extent
to which it is contestable (through its myth of the individual, of the
associative contractual relation, through its construction of 'happiness'
as a final end, and so on), if they cannot consequently claim universally
to teach how to live (by requiring that their ethics would be preferred to
any other), they are nevertheless an irreplaceable instrument for saying
'no' and for protesting: placing a safety catch on the unacceptable and
jamming the door against them.[5]

As a *tool* that is indefinitely reconfigurable (which is why their
Declaration gets re-written at each new historical moment) as well as
being at the same time transculturally unlimited (since they raise a de-
contextualisable and 'denuded' protest, solely in the name of the *being
who was born*), human rights precisely give a name to this 'in the name of
what': a final recourse which, without them, would remain nameless and
therefore would leave us without a capacity to intervene and to protest.
The fact that this *negative*, and insurrectional, function gets the better of
the positive dimension of the notion, joins with the more general function which I consider to constitute the vocation of the universal: that of
reopening a breach in all confining and satisfied totality, and reviving the
aspiration towards it. Isn't the fact easily observable? All of those who,
the world over, today invoke human rights do not, for all that, adhere to
Western ideology (do they even know what it is?); but they find in these
'human rights' the ultimate argument or rather instrument, endlessly
passed from hand to hand and available for any future cause, not so much

to outline a new form of opposition – of which one can always suspect that it still makes common cause with its partner – adversary – as (more radically) *to refuse*: bringing about the vivid appearance of an operational, non-integrated and non-alienated transcendence in the immanence of every situation. Although the opposition is always diverse because it is oriented by its context, the refusal is initially dissociated from what it rejects and is valued as a unique gesture – opening out suddenly onto the unconditioned by nakedly shouting out what I earlier evoked, by way of a final and even unsurpassable notion, as the common meaning of the human. On their negative sides, human rights would then succeed in expressing *in an exemplary way* this universality of refusal.

4 If I earlier got as far as dealing with the 'universalizing' capacity of human rights, it was because in the end I needed to extricate myself a little from our usual terms: to mark conceptually a divergence in relation to expected and acknowledged (and, because of this, tested) conceptions of the universal. For, faced with the question of their status, don't we find human rights insidiously out of plumb – making it necessary therefore to start by straightening them out? Failing to do so would entail the risk of sinking into vain discussion and not completely being able to extricate oneself from the familiar contradictions around which we see so many debates turn today: having no other alternative than to demand an arrogant universality of human rights and condemning us to mistake, in a denial which is mortal to them, the extent to which they are culturally marked – not only in their historical emergence, but also in the notional and civilizational prejudices from which they have emerged – or to abandon, through theoretical pique, the insurrectional weapon of protest they constitute and which can *a priori* serve universally today in every place on our planet – in this they remain, to this day, without any equivalent or possible replacement. This is the risk, as I say, of otherwise inevitably falling back into one or the other of these opposed ruts: of lowering one's aim from the absoluteness of their imperative [*devoir-être*] (and no longer being able to pose them as intangible principles) *or* naively (or in a cunning way) making them the basic *credo* of the new globalized order (and inevitably because of this once again renewing Western imperialism).

In dealing with *universalizing*, I am opening up a deviation in our words with a view to expressing two things at once: (1) instead of assuming a universality to human rights which they would possess from the outset, through a sort of conceptual inneism, or transcendentalism, inspired by that of human nature, *universalizing* suggests, through its gerund, that the universal is to be found there underway, on the move, in process (which is not yet concluded): on the way to being realized; (2) at the same time, instead of allowing itself be conceived as a property or a passively possessed quality, universalizing gives us to understand that it is a factor, an agent or a promoter: that it is in itself a vector of the universal, and not by reference to and under the dependency of some instituted representation – that it is therefore no longer to be gauged, as is ordinarily done, by the possible extension of a truth. What I therefore understand by the universalizing capacity of human rights is that they engage or *effect the emergence* of the universal; that, through their particular skylight, historically and ideologically delineated, they reveal and put to work its 'regulating' principle – which is really the only transcendental I might recognize.

For in the end the question is really this: is it or is it not necessary (and on what basis as well as on what level?) to maintain a cultural (or 'transcendental') *unconditional*? I would, for my part, pose it on the sole basis and level of this (strictly functional, and not notional – or 'constitutive') *regulating* principle of the universal. This means, in this case, that human rights are not in themselves universal (the singularity of their appearance reveals this), but that their *lack* or loss causes a genuinely intense universal of humanity to arise, one that is transcultural and trans-historical and which I would otherwise be unable to name, but in whose name I can, *a priori*, reject and legitimately protest against everything which calls them into question, no matter what the cultural context.

Why then do our conceptions of the universal, as inherited from classical philosophy put us out of kilter in our thinking about human rights if it's not that they only awkwardly enable us to envisage the status of human rights on a level that does not belong to them, and this in a double sense? They make us consider them from a point of view that is cognitive (derived from the traditional theory of knowledge) at the same time as it is positive, as a content of statements which should be examined to determine whether the allegiance they require is in itself legitimate. The universalizing character of human rights is then of the order not of knowing (of the theoretical) but of the operational (or of the practical): we invoke them (they intervene) in order to act, from the outset, on *any* given situation. On the other hand, their extension is not of the order of some *credo* (of an ideological nature) in which we are commanded to place our trust, but is understood (negatively) as what their lack alone reveals suddenly that is *a priori* (or unconditioned) at the very heart of our experience; and therefore as that upon which we should unconditionally lean so as to open a resistance: it is of the order not of truth, but of an appeal.

In this it is necessary to distinguish the *universalizing* from the *universalisable*; what separates them is precisely such a difference of level. The universalisable is what makes a claim to the quality of universality, as a statement of truth. Thus it inevitably encounters the prickly problem of its possibility [*pouvoir être*]:[6] having to justify in what name this extension it assumes is legitimate, the universalisable always risks being charged with being excessively pretentious for according itself more than what it has a right to (since it is not the proven universal), and of being considered as fraudulent, or at least as contentious. As for *universalizing*, it is indemnified from this problem of legitimacy: since it is what causes the universal to arise (by default and in an operative way); it does not claim but creates, and its value is measured by the power and intensity of this effect. Thus we can say that human rights are a strong or effective *universalizing* force. For the question, when it comes to human rights, is no longer one of knowing whether they are universalizable – in other words whether they can be proposed as a statement of truth for all cultures in the world (rather, in this case, the answer is no) – but really to ensure that they produce an *effect* of the universal serving as unconditional (such is their function as a weapon or negative tool) in whose name a struggle, a legitimate resistance, is justified *a priori*.

> Needless to say it is necessary for me to distinguish such a *universalizing* from the 'principle of universalization' (*Universalisierungsgrundsatz*) by which Jürgen Habermas undertook to found the legitimacy of norms commanding moral actions in reason (2001: 63). For if he separates constative speech acts

(relating to facts) on the one hand and regulative ones (relating to interpersonal relations) on the other – in other words, propositional truth on the one side and normative correctness on the other, or the demands of truth and those of validity, he no less considers the latter on the scale of the former (which moreover is justified in the cognitivist option which is his own in order to discredit any sceptical attitude in relation to values). Thus he conceives of the principle of universalization required in moral argumentation as a principle playing a role equivalent to that of the principle of induction, so allowing it, in the discourse of knowledge, to move from singular observations to universal hypotheses and thereby to seal the rift between them. But it is precisely this analogue of the principle of induction which by generalization passes from one to the other, or rather from the one to all, and which thereby acts as a 'bridge' (*als Brückenprinzip*) from the individual to the universal that seems suspect to me. It does not appear to resist the fact that, in its argumentative form, the disparity of cultures and the mutual *indifference* of their conceptions brings to the fore a completely different problem, one unsuspected by Kantianism, such that precisely the European genealogy of human rights makes us measure them. In this new light, one can no longer be content to think of the universal as the 'impartial' or the 'impersonal', since every concerned person is constrained by the demands of linguistic engagement to adopt the perspective of all others, just as Habermas does in his ethical project founded on communication. But, when confronting it with the cultural unthought, it is necessary to detach the universal more radically from the level of representation. No longer should we seek a notional extensivity for it which would always risk being placed in peril in other cultures, but we should attach ourselves to the unconditional that its *lack* (such is indeed the case when human rights are lacking) suddenly reveals.

Can (European) human rights alone be cited as *universalizing*, however? In fact, I recall that the need to reconsider the universal from this angle first of all occurred to me from reading Mencius. Let's consider the case of someone suddenly noticing a child on the point of falling into a well (the example chosen by Mencius), who is immediately overcome with terror and reaches out to grab the child (not because he has a privileged relation with its parents, or because he wants to be rewarded, or because he would be blamed if he did not . . .): this gesture eludes us and is completely reactive; we cannot fail to do it. Mencius then continues (II, A, 6): 'Whoever does not have such a [moral] consciousness of pity [as a feeling of something intolerable at the sight of the bad things that happen to others: to translate it by 'pity', in this context is, I recognise, far too doloristic] is not a man.' In short, anyone who would not have reached out 'is not a man'. Rather than starting out with a definition which would necessarily be ideologically determined and, because of this, singular, Mencius highlights (and does so *negatively*, from his inadmissible lack) what, in itself, as an uncontrolled reaction of 'humanity', has universality as a vocation. It is therefore not a question here of something 'universalizable', of the order of representation, whose possible extensivity should be validated as a statement of truth; but involves, as something *universalizing*, this irrepressible *refusal*: to allow the child to fall into the well. Moreover, 'Man' here is only in a position of a predicate, not of a subject: for the 'being-man' is *formed* by having such a consciousness of pity.

What nonetheless separates this *case*, from which Mencius draws his moral lesson, from the concept of human rights in that human rights benefit from a status of abstraction which renders them transculturally operative (which is what accounts for their unequalled availability to intervene in every situation that is encountered). What is more, they deliberately engage in a political resistance, confronted with oppression, that is hardly ever to be found among Chinese thinkers. It remains the case that Mencius manages to conjure up in terms of *universalizing*, bringing the universal to the surface at the level of experience – such is really his image (that of an 'end' that suddenly appears) – an unconditional quality of the human which can be affirmed *a priori* to be shared across cultures. More bluntly still: this cry that one makes (that hand one reaches out) upon seeing this small child tottering, on the point of falling into the well, is of course obvious, with no need of cultural interpretation or mediation, that ('intrinsic' – *ben*, the Chinese says) of the *common meaning of the human* (that is, the notion of *ren*). In other words, taking into account the disparity of cultures, and the way in which it forces us to flush out the unthought of our thinking, does not, for all that, entail abandoning the exigency of the common. We still need to agree upon the way in which the 'common' should be conceived.

XI From where is the common derived if it is neither synthesis, denominator nor foundation?

1 The commonality [*commun*] of cultures is most often envisaged according to these facile imaginations and inverted games: either one assembles or isolates; either one marries together or separates out. Either one dreams of a synthesis of cultures by placing in common what is completed in it or, alternatively, separates them out and, distinguishing what would be identical in them, retains only their shared denominator. The first approach bears within it an ambition of auspicious understanding, born of totalization, and rests on the old myth of the binary relation in which one thing is offered complacently to the other: thus it particularly favours setting up the 'Orient' and the 'Occident' as poles of human experience – 'East and West', the great symbolic marriage.[1] Take the question of 'time': through its analytical clarity, we are told (by Wu Kuang-ming, one of the most high-profile Chinese intellectuals in the United States) that the West has furnished the rigorous, 'fundamental' concept of time as a universal tool (*a basic, primitive or primary concept* – as obvious (indispensable) as 'A is A' is what he says in evidence); China, for its part, has furnished its 'flesh and blood' by illuminating 'lived time' (Wu Kuang-ming, 1998: 342). Thereby the two are called upon in marriage: the abstract and the objective on the one hand (the 'West' of reason), the concrete and the subjective on the other (the 'Orient' of intuition). The one is 'ovule' and the other 'seed'; China is *yin*, the West *yang*: could what forms the mystery of the 'cross-fertilization' between cultures be more eloquently represented?

But how are these purveyors of great cultural symbiosis unable to see that they are thinking about the difference of cultures only in Western terms? They are so numerous today (the idea is even close to becoming a dogma on the West coast), especially among Americanized Chinese who, even when expressing themselves in Chinese, speak in terms of 'concrete'/'abstract', 'subject'/'object' and so on. Consequently, they conceive of their own culture only in the other's terms, making it a mere reflection, and one which acts in its likeness? The community of cultures appears to be a lot better guaranteed in the future if they are all already perceived, through the European conceptual medium, only as simple exotic variants of the Western. For according to what other pre-established harmony would they emerge from their heterotopia and initial disparity to come to fit together *in fine*, as surely as in a jigsaw puzzle, no matter what the strange shape of their respective elements might be? What overall design would they thereby be able to achieve other than that pre-defining one of the initially established (European) human sciences? Even the renowned 'cross-fertilization' between cultures, if one is satisfied with this image, stems from ever more singular gestations, ever more oblique and elaborate (*invented*) strategies, rather than from simple contact and from worlds embracing one another.

This is what is nevertheless announced by these formulae with all the appeal of ready-made catch-phrases, which are so convenient ideologically: 'The third millennium, it is decided, will be that of synthesis, or will not be.' The tone is in fact that of a millenarian prophecy: 'In this way our homo-ecological symbiosis will finally happen and we will truly enjoy together our global cultural togetherness' (Wu Kuang-ming, 1998: 342). At least there is the free re-enactment of the happy ending learned from political summits (the familiar reconciliatory 'statements of consensus' promoted at the end of stormy discussions): the new globalized culture is now represented in the Parliament of the world which promises to the democratic integration of every diverse current (it is unable not to do so . . .). The cultural citizen of the world of the future has even often been described as someone who will do his shopping in a superstore, in that sort of world 'supermarket' of culture, and will choose what he likes from the products on display, going from one aisle to another, placing his choices in his shopping trolley . . . But the image is false: cultural notions and representations are not dissociable from their context in this way. They cannot be arranged side by side, shelved according to their 'rationalism', 'hedonism' or 'salvation' (a bit of *zen* here – a bit of Epicureanism there – a bit of negative theology – a bit of . . ., and you can organize your happiness as soon as you get home). How can we fail to take into account that these aisles have been organized and erected only according to the categories of European reason: that it is the now globalized Western culture which has designed the packaging, the way things should be classified right down to the labelling used, and it has even set up every last patch of this department-store-*cum*-grand-bazaar – henceforth fitted out as they all are, with their aisles tagged for consumption?

The other side of the synthesis is analysis: we will break down beliefs and religions into primary elements (everything ideological that the contemporary world now brings into communication) so as to discern what corresponds. Since it is unable to present itself as an identical, solid core, the common can be located in this, at least as a comparable relation between terms, an analogous form of intersection or mediation.[2] Since the nineties, UNESCO has worked a lot on this identification of points of understanding. It has done so by contributing to the formulation of a 'global' or 'planetary' ethic, since it is supposed to favour peaceful relations between cultures. Once more the tone (for the *tone* here is also eminently part of it) is still that of the solemn Declaration: 'We confirm that there is already a consensus among the religions which can be the basis for a global ethic – a minimal fundamental consensus concerning binding values, irrevocable standards, and fundamental moral attitudes . . .' (see, for example, Küng and Kuschel, 1997: 18). I would refrain from translating the original into French, since the terms are again not only once those of standardized Western (in other words, Americanized) language – 'hopes, goals, ideals . . .' – but are equally very difficult to detach from idiosyncratic liaisons and phrases (even from what one imagines were the accents and intonations) used in this type of *meeting* (if I were to translate it into French, there would really be nothing left of it . . .).

So let us once more compare this with the initial age of globalization which (for the West) was the Roman Empire. Let's measure both: what the Latin jurists, faced with the influx of all those who came to live in Rome and were not subject to Roman law, codified in their *jus gentium*, 'right of nations', as a sort of smallest common denominator of the usages of all known peoples, and, consequently, as what would seem closest to justice for the greatest number, something which at least had the merit of being directly useful for the establishment of social life. They did not make a claim to a pre-established principle of truth, but sought only to render this very diverse cohabitation of morals and beliefs legally viable. This effectively served to enact the law. And, unlike the eulogists of a worldwide ethics today, it did not seek to hide the element of *construction* that any enterprise in which one would be limited to collecting together and making an inventory of the common still inevitably preserves (and which occurs through the very language and tools with which this inventory is made).

For it is said over and over today, in projects of *Global Ethics*, as a minimal but incontestable ingredient, that all moral traditions and all religions the world over advocate peace ('a vision of peoples living peacefully together' – Küng and Kuschel, 1997: 18) – and who therefore would dare to assert that peace is not desirable? However, can we forget that Heraclitus among the Greeks and Hegel among the moderns, to name but two, *have needed* to think through the instigating logic of war so as to emphasize the function of the negative, including its ethical elements. This is precisely what immediately reveals the whole of this contemporary deployment of good conscience for what it is: a fearful incapacity to take responsibility for the *negative*, in other words to think about and isolate from purely destructive negation what its fertile and inventive use could be. In the age of consensual standardizations, I even see the intellectual's principal work in this intelligence of the negative and its promising, but not yet identified, paths (see Jullien 2004: 16). I am moreover amazed that the promoters of all of these religious forums and Davos summits of culture have not thought more about how little interest their work has aroused, once the effect of its proclamation has worn off (I exclude UNESCO, whose forced and state-sponsored interest this is).[3] Why therefore has *The Declaration Toward a Global Ethic* (of the Parliament of the religions of the world, 1993) not had the same impact as the *Universal Declaration of Human Rights* which the text nevertheless claimed to emulate? It is because human rights are a concept which, culturally – rather than ecumenically – marked as it is, is no less a strong concept, as I have said, whose negative side, that of resistance, of value at least as a universalizing force, possesses a resolve which is not about to be blunted. Inversely, the 'global ethic' is nothing but a collection of truisms. These *truisms* are without either interest or effect; they are not even 'true'. In any event, they do not make History.

And yet what has happened to the 'golden rule'? Doesn't that at least contain a fine consensus among civilizations? We read it twice over in the *Analects* of Confucius (IV, 15; XV, 23): 'Zigong asked: "Is there one word one should put in practice throughout one's life?" The Master replied: "Might it be reciprocity? One should not do to others what one does not want done to oneself"' (see Mencius, IV, A, 9). This statement is then found in both the Old (The Book of Tobias, 4, 15a) and New Testaments (the Sermon on the Mount) but equally in Isocrates and the Emperor Severus Alexander (on the pediment of his palace is written: '*Quod tibi fieri non vis, alteri ne feceris*'); and it is not difficult to continue this list through Islam, Buddhism and Hinduism.

Of the *minima moralia* common to all humanity, this would be the most authentic. Nevertheless, as German colleagues Ulrich Unger and G. Wohlfart have analysed, even this basic, most elementary, formula reveals a singular dimension in the context of the *Analects* (see Unger, 2003: 19-41). Instead of being presented as an, or rather as *the*, obliged precept, it emerges from an exchange of words between kith and kin, and Confucius proposes it only as a possible path of reflection; rather than serving as an abstract maxim, a prefiguration of the categorical imperative, it remains imprinted with the Chinese meaning of resonance or responsivity (*gan-yang*) according to which the ethical is not separated from the affective, and such that all beings are perceived as originally in interaction and vibration with one another (similar to how the ancient Greek also expressed it by 'sym-pathetic'). To deprive it of this would be to ossify it as so many 'irrevocable standards' of the contemporary world discourse are stiffened, stereotyped and rendered insignificant.

2 Because the *complementarity* of cultures is planned from the outset, it always runs the risk of proceeding from a fantasy, that of ecumenicalism and reconciliation, at the same time as it is nothing but the product of a preliminary assimilation, operating secretly and remaining unsuspected, from which then derives, on a single categorical ground, the illusion of a fortunate matching: its *commonality* [*commun*] has every reason to be contrived. As for *cross-referencing* between cultures, it always risks being superficial since, as it necessarily proceeds from the exterior of the thing,

it is never certain to affect the individual. Faced with these common elements, gleaned here and there in the diversity of civilizations, could a more solid commonality [*commun*], which would be that of Reason, therefore be advanced? Or, to get away from these effects of perspective and play of surfaces, how could the common, between people as well as between cultures, find its more fundamental place and justify what is required of it? This is what contemporary rationalism, associated with Apel and Habermas, has tried to do: for a more solid commonality [*commun*] to be established, one that would even be indisputable, nothing could be more convincing than to conjure it up from the very rules of language conceived as *communication* and serving it as a 'basis'.

> Let us therefore, we are asked, relinquish the traditional paradigms of philosophy, those of the truth-correspondence (in ontology) or the truth-evidence (in the philosophy of reflective consciousness and the transcendental subject), so as to perceive, without taking into account the question of the conditions of knowledge, that the community between people, as a *communicational community*, is to be sought directly at the level of the conditions of possibility of meaningful discourse (Apel, 1981: 895). In fact, the rules of language use are rules whose validity has always implicitly been recognized from the moment one speaks, therefore they are what every person shares *a priori*. It is consequently in the activity of communication through the word alone that, among all people – even as soon as there are people – in any place as at any moment of human history, what will really need to be recognized as the *transcendental* of the common is tested and verified. For, as soon as one speaks, to oneself as to others, one pragmatically puts this transcendental to work (*a priori*) and cannot do otherwise. Let us therefore reverse the traditional order of the parts of philosophy, as Apel enjoins us; the common that ethics seeks to promote is no longer to be constructed *after* the logic whose rigour ethics would seek to conserve (but isn't this in vain?), but we see on the contrary that logic itself assumes this ethic (of the common) which is a pre-requisite of communication. Or, if an appeal is still made to *consensus*, then this is no longer, as before, the object of more or less uncertain ideological operations or ones shot through with good intentions: since its exigency is given to us and guides

us *a priori* through those rules that all discourse forces us to share and from which it *is impossible* for anyone, even when speaking to themselves, to escape.

The *common* will be therefore not so much *what* people could ever express, by way of 'content', or else (and this includes all of their statements of consensus and vows of understanding) it will always be so only in a secondary way. They will never do anything but make explicit at the level of intentions or conceptions this commonality which from the very start is formally implicated and is given to us as what is most innate: the simple possibility of speaking in a *meaningful way*. For it is enough that they speak, no matter what it is they say: by the fact of its status as at once pragmatic and transcendental, this commonality is attested to by the slightest word at the same time as no earlier principle could have given an account of it – with it we actually touch the 'final basis' of reason. This is what Aristotle was already showing about the principle of non-contradiction being introduced as the first rule of any *logos*, its first axiom, founding the 'speech community', *koinônia logou*: on the one hand, this principle cannot be justified without itself already being implicated in this justification, which inevitably leads to a *petitio principii*; but, at the same time, the adversary of this principle of non-contradiction cannot undertake to refute it without himself putting it to work as soon as he says something and introduces a meaningful form of speaking, and so he subscribes to it himself and, consequently, contradicts himself. Whether one might wish to justify or refute it, this principle is always *pre-supposed*, and whoever 'undertakes to destroy the *logos*', 'still supports it' (*Metaphysics*, 'Gamma', 3-4). For, as soon as he speaks, he finds he has to submit to these rules of the word and so participates *de facto* in the community of those who speak and signify. Otherwise, excluding himself from the common, he at the same time excludes himself from humanity – and sinks into inhumanity. He becomes 'like a plant', Aristotle says; this means suicide, says Apel.

So should we be satisfied with this? For anyone who wants to found the common through reason, doesn't the question inevitably come back to the 'transcendental' of communication: even conceived in an ideal mode, would the communicational community towards which one leans by implicitly accepting its rules completely resist the divergence of cultures? Since the point of view required here is so pragmatic, I have no hesitation in bringing my own practice as a sinologist into play with a view to discussing the issue. Isn't it, moreover, perhaps through a lack of 'philology', in the sense in which Nietzsche understood it, that, with too much confidence in linguistic generality, this conception would first fish for answers? What I am asking is whether, between the European and the Chinese (to confine myself to this relation), it might want to respect equally the (same) *a-priori* pre-conditions of argumentation and still, speaking in the language of the one, but which the other knows, find ourselves betrayed by this medium and prevented from effective understanding? Even worse than this: we can think are in agreement with the other, between cultures, without even suspecting the extent to which we have made mistakes about it and do not understand it. Apel goes straight to the conditions required from the outset by the word, but has he taken sufficient account of the depth of what is implicit within what has amassed in language and from which an idiomatic singularity is born? Moreover, I would ask whether this communicational community has been conceived in terms of more properly argumentative pre-expectations, those which European thought has privileged, and which are therefore completely relevant only if one is starting from that basis. Not that, properly speaking, other cultures are necessarily unaware of them, but perhaps they discreetly sidestep their demands or at least maintain a looser link with them, one that is less constraining and favours other modalities of the word.

The first case is what we constantly experience, especially between cultures which have developed without having shared any relations of language or history. To take one example: I translate (I can only translate) *shen* (in Chinese; *kami* in Japanese) by *esprit*[4] ('the spiritual') but, in doing so, I mobilize on both sides some latent parts of signification which only partially correspond and whose confusion leads one astray (or, to use a previous example, if I translate *tian* by 'sky/heaven', 'celestial', or *tian shi* as 'celestial food', which is in fact the only possible translation – see Jullien, 2006). I even point this out all the time when I am teaching: the Chinese text is correctly translated, and cannot even be translated in any other way, but, for all that, it does not mean in French what it does in

Chinese (Jullien, 2006: 148). For what is the correct way of 'sharing linguistic meaning' as Apel says, going back to Aristotle who placed upon himself as his first requisite the requirement that words should have the same meaning? It is only after a slow and patient maturing at the heart of the other culture, according to what I have earlier called the 'profession', that we progressively learn to take account of misunderstandings and can even begin to measure them and mentally reduce the divergence while necessarily continuing to translate in this way – it is not a question here simply of making adjustments. The predicament we face consequently has nothing to do with what linguists call the perlocutary, and which Apel takes into consideration: that the interlocutor might very well not be able to understand everything even while having perfect command of the language, because the statement then serves more distant ends (it aims at rendering a service or at hindering and so on). But Apel insists that it should really be recognized as something culturally *implicit* which, as such, has endless ramifications, and thereby prevents him from hoping to reach, in this way, any 'ground' or 'basis' whatever. In this sense, the subjacent language is also, because of this fact, in its own way 'sub-ject', and not only (conveniently) a medium: language (*a* language) thereby speaks to a certain extent, in a preliminary way, through me. Likewise, the equivalent proposed by the translation of only being able to sidestep it needs a whole process of familiarization, which is moreover never concluded, in order gradually to enter this other unity, to take part in its secret intelligibility, and to do so while working against the adopted tradition.

Moreover, shouldn't it be necessary to cite in the first place the claim to truth said not only to be directly linked to propositions by means of assertoric speech acts, but also to be indirectly linked to all other types of speech acts in the form of existential pre-suppositions, on the basis of pre-expectations, which form a fold and secretly orient what Apel understands by 'communication'. These appear to me too narrow in regard to other cultures. I therefore wonder if this is precisely true in relation, for example, to the *Analects* of Confucius. They aim at 'inciting', giving a finishing touch to the disciple by 'putting him on the path' (of wisdom), and they were conceived 'in an apposite way', *ad hominem* – they are content to give an immediate indication and they barely express anything (see, for example, XI, 21). This is why Confucius can respond differently to the same question depending on the person, indeed differently to the same person, without this creating a problem (see 'On Filial Piety', II, 5-6-7-8). His argument varies opportunely according to the moment so as to reveal each time what is, in its adequacy which cannot be codified to the situation, the consistent exigency of conduct (the meaning of *zhong*, the 'middle', understood as *regulation*) – he does not 'express' the truth.

> This point is crucial and should be carefully considered. For I am not saying that Confucius 'makes no claim to the truth', or that he would have been indifferent to it, if the question were to be posed to him, but that it is certainly *not from this angle* that he conceives his words. To introduce the notion of truth here, even of an 'existential proposition' in the most discreet way, falsifies the perspective by bringing the topic of wisdom (as it extends from Confucius to the remarks of the Zen masters) back under the philosophical injunction. His problem, in contrast to what we are told about Socrates, is not one of the definitions of essences. Similarly he does not aim to make declarations. This is moreover why the *Analects* are so disappointing on (first) reading, causing so many Europeans, with Hegel (2006: 107-8) at their head, to find them insipid (on the other hand, the great Japanese sinologist Yoshikawa Kojiro said they constituted 'the most beautiful book in the world'): we will find almost nothing in them by way of the propositional, or, if we do, then it is only as a truism. At the same time they only rarely respond to strategic ends (according to Apel's distinction between 'communicational consensus' and 'secretly strategic communication'). But by dint of reading and re-reading them, by memorizing and 'savouring' them, we can perceive in these 'subtle remarks' (*wei yan*) an *indexical* value which is always *vivid* (*huo yu*), which does not get bogged down in lessons and, in its availability, 'could not be exhausted'. In other words, we need to allow the unlimited impact of what they contain, which in truth is not so much meaning as 'stimulation', to emanate from the slightest formula, so that each reading reveals a glimpse of the 'globality' of wisdom that they contain.

In the same way, when Apel considers equal rights and duties to be presupposed in the reciprocity of argumentation, by way of ideal norms of communication, I wonder, once again, if the topic of wisdom responds to such a preoccupation, and if it even 'pre-supposes' it. In the Far East at least, the master–disciple relation may be surreptitiously deviant in relation to this rights–duties equality posed in principle. Equally, from the European side, we may still be within a protocol of dialogue like the one Socrates established in order to found the democratic *homologia* but which is out of kilter as soon as we open the *Analects*. The reciprocity in argumentation within it is routinely *skewed* (see the occasion when Confucius refuses to argue with Zilu – *Analects* XI, 24) and so the topic of wisdom appears to work in the margin (or rather in ignorance, or disdain) of such a need for equality. It is hardly concerned with it at all. For the problem Apel keeps in mind (in fact, which has continued from Aristotle to Apel) is one of convincing the sceptic of the universalism of reason and justifying its possible foundation. Therefore, *paying no heed to* Apel's stipulations, as the topic of wisdom in ancient China did, is something completely different from casting doubt on them and giving proof of scepticism. This is therefore why anyone satisfied with such stipulations, as *a-priori* communicational norms, if reading the *Analects* of Confucius in a standard way, will find in their topics nothing more than a poor, colourless and flat (because not constructed) facsimile of our philosophy – ordinarily compensated for only after the event by bringing exoticism into play. Constrained to pass beneath these Caudine Forks, they have now in effect become insipid, as Hegel said in criticizing their Chinese 'savour', and have no more interest than any moralism.

3 Let's take a step back. Habermas is conscious of the fact that to found the commonality [*commun*] of reason from the implicit rules of argumentation would be to incur the criticism of ethnocentrism. Moreover, European philosophy in the end wonders whether the fact that 'the norms and actions which incarnate universalisable interests' are the only ones which 'correspond to the way in which we conceive justice'. So doesn't this constitute a particular point of view, appropriate to Western culture alone? This constitutes a new 'paralogism' of reason, one neglected by Kant but which the testimony of anthropologists has finally made apparent. Habermas also falls back on the transcendental demand projected at the source of the common. This meant that meaning and its

consensual regime, which themselves only make demands for want of a rule of replacement, could not from that moment forth be recognized (secured) except by and in *discussion*. As it finally aims to produce conviction and subjective agreement by leading the listener through reason (*durch Gründe*) to accept the exigency of truth attached to the affirmation advanced, this ethic of communication is the only one that is reliable. These rules of discussion, *Diskursregeln*, alone take us out of the realm of conventions into what are really 'inescapable pre-suppositions' (1983: 89).

Then, just as the *Analects* of Confucius impel us to break out of the straitjacket of argumentative rules (or else, if they were read according to the prescription given by such rules, they would lose all relief), isn't this ethic of discussion still too narrow, conceived as it is by maintaining an attachment (also profoundly Greek) to the virtue of the word? In any case it seems unreliable to me, and a lot less inescapable than we have been led to believe, as soon as I consider it from the 'speaking without speaking' (*yan wu yan*) of the Taoists (see *Zhuangzi*, ch. 27 – Guo Quinfan, n.d.: 949). Haven't they taught us that we can very well speak for the whole day among ourselves, and even for the whole of our life, 'without ever having said anything': maintaining ourselves in each other's intimacy, linked one to the other through an uninterrupted word, but without ever 'saying' anything, in fact – without ever demonstrating the desire to produce a 'meaning'; without anything, by the evening, deserving to be remembered as having been 'expressed'? Just as one can in 'not speaking, not have not spoken' (*Zhuangzi*, ibid.; see also Jullien, 2006: 159). We have not thereby ceased to understand each other; both of us maintain a mutual intelligence, without anything having to be spoken, without a need for any recourse to obvious signs, and with this silence itself not being 'eloquent' . . .

> The *conviction*, *Überzeugung*, on which Habermas founds himself as on an ultimate but unshakeable rock, really appears, in fact, viewed from China, to be a 'Greek thing'. In any case, convincing others is not a Taoist ambition, and the Taoist hardly ever even conceives of it. But to say 'scarcely', 'on the side', 'at will', and even to speak (listen) 'extravagantly', represent an art which plays out what the Greeks (Socrates) admirably defined as the persua-

sive demand we find at work in dialogue. One will likewise quite naturally sidestep the constraints of communication that appear so petty; even the rules and the whole protocol of discussion are disdained. Or 'how could I find someone who forgets what it is to speak?', says Zhuangzi, and 'speak with him' (ch. 26 – Guo Quinfan, n.d.: 944). To produce an 'inter-subjective agreement', as invoked by Habermas, this speaking without speaking does not submit to the determination of a 'meaning', does not have an 'object', it no longer has anything aimed at or assigned, but it aspires to an understanding that is implicit as well as immediate ('intuitive' we usually say for convenience) which, as such, extends to others in a stirring and discreet way, is 'beyond words' (*yan wai*) and without concern for the all-too artificial pretensions of truth.

To defend this ethic of discussion, which is the only thing upon which the common will be constructed, Habermas joins Apel in showing how his opponent contradicts himself, *de facto*, in the act or 'performatively': whoever refuses to subscribe to the *a-priori* rules of argumentation, as Apel showed (and as Aristotle already had), is nonetheless constrained to have recourse to it as soon as he argues against them. It is the same with Habermas: he will agree to enter into discussion with any Sophist who refuses to admit these *a-priori* ethics in order to show him, catching him in the act, that he is always already himself in the process of betraying his declared position by his actions, since he too requires conviction. Indeed, just by the fact that he remains implicated in lived relations, as he cannot fail to be, he never ceases performatively to make an appeal (all day long) to the very thing he claims to abolish: 'as long as he is still alive *at all*' the sceptic can only give in to a 'Robinson Crusoe' type of muteness, Habermas decisively states, that 'does not even reach the degree of representability of a sham experiment' (Habermas, 1990: 100).[5] From this, we return to the dilemma: either prior adhesion to the requisites of 'reason', always previously assumed, or exclusion from humanity.

The question raised is precisely this: since the Taoist would avoid occupying a 'sceptical' position *vis-à-vis* that of the cognitivist, will he allow himself to be caught in the trap of such a 'pragmatico-transcendental' contradiction? For he lends himself *equally* to the discussion, and doesn't even dream of making a claim against it. Yet for all that he does not make it a constraint: he is not concerned with applying himself to doubting its pertinence, but considers it as merely opportune (see Jullien, 2001: 117). He no more submits to the principle of non-contradiction than he abandons it – why would one allow oneself to be caught within this dilemma? And can't one release its grip? Why wouldn't one conduct oneself in this as in everything else, by evolving 'according to the moment' or 'at will'? (See Mencius on Confucius: 'He is the moment of wisdom' (V, B, 1).) 'Once one has banished the disjunction [between true and false, between good and bad], one has also banished this banishment [of the disjunction]' (Guo Xiang, commenting on Zhuangzi, in Guo Qingfan, n.d.: 79; see Jullien, 1998: 138). Just as he 'is busy without being busy' or 'savours the lack of savour', so the Sage is the prisoner of neither. And so he neither allows himself to be constrained by the logic of exclusion, nor does he deprive himself of this resource. He no more 'attaches' himself to it than he 'leaves' it. Such is the 'pivot' of the door, it remains open to the one as to the other, to its use as to its non-use, and such is really its 'great use' (*da yong*) whose 'extent' expresses here the fact that it is not exclusive. Between the losses entailed from one thing and another, from that of submission and that of abandonment, doesn't a play remain in relation to them, such that it renders the Sage eminently *available*? While Apel or Habermas *cannot imagine* emerging from their Aristotelian principle of the excluded middle, we see that the alternative which Western reason, ever since Aristotle, has been so good at enhancing is dissolved (not resolved) in this 'accord' of the Taoists, as it maintains an equal opening to both (either one submits to the commonality [*commun*] of communicational reason, regulated *a priori* as it is, or all possible community is definitively lost).

4 From the beginning, Apel and Habermas concur on this question of how to save ethics from the hydra of irrationalism when Kantian autonomy no longer seems sufficient. The only way they envisage of escaping the impasses of the formalism of morality, while falling short of doing so, lies in seeking universality in the very regulating of language conceived as communication. But, as soon as one begins to think outside of the European context, would such *regulating* not itself be arbitrary, or

at least culturally marked? In other words, would it not be due to *logos* alone, as shown by the texts of wisdom in ancient China (among other examples, no doubt – I am basing this only on my own readings) easily overflowing these imposed conditions, naturally and without remorse, on their Confucian or Taoist side? For how can we ever be sure of having overcome what has come before, what was first there in the beginning and established a lineage? How could I ever be assured of having sufficiently traced back on this side of the divergence of cultures to be able finally to lay bare the *a-priori* basis of reason?

Therefore the path appears to me rather to be continued in the opposite direction: precisely by going back once more to Kant, but again this time in an oblique way. In other words, the commonality [*commun*] of humanity needs to be tackled, not directly from the point of view of ethics, that of practical reason, but by cutting across, as I have started to do, those of knowledge and judgement (in the two other *Critiques*) – put differently, by re-envisaging the communication from which the common comes, no longer from the angle of normative and as such prerequisite constraints, but by way of a *capacity* arising from a power of the faculties. This will be done not by way of implied regulations, which always risk the observation that they are ignored elsewhere or that one can easily do without them, but by way of an indefinitely shareable possibility [*pouvoir être*] – the very one I started to evoke, following Kant, as *universal communicability*. Consequently, what is needed is to start not from a final metamorphosis of more refined innateness, but from what will be posed as resolutely prospective. This means that knowledge and judgements 'must be able', Kant tells us, to 'be communicated [or 'shared'] universally', '*müssen sich [. . .] allgemein mitteilen lassen*' (1978: 21).

In fact, it seems to me that the common of humanity *is not held* (which would be of the order of the base or the reference). It neither arises from it, nor remains attached to it. It does not hold to rules or norms which we would see ourselves from the outset as having been subject to (the Rule of the Good or the Beautiful or even those rules of 'judicious discourse'). For we will always suspect that they again enclose this common in the communitarian, since this question will always have to be asked when drawing up its genealogy: are their codes not codifications (and as such always threatened with an exception and conversely liable to provoke all the more violently the anathema of exclusion. As much appears symptomatically in a striking continuity which, from Aristotle to Habermas, is usually rather immovable: anyone who does not respect judicious discourse has ceased to be anything more than a plant, is constrained to suicide and excluded from humanity . . . On the contrary, I say that this commonality [*commun*] of the human belongs to the order of the source. It 'comes', and never ceases to come, from what alone forms an inexhaustible *resource*. The common is not the base, as the French speak of the base of a case (*fundus*) which is finally revealed when everything has been taken out of it; when all of the differences between cultures have been removed (and abstracted). But it is the basic funds (*fons*) in the sense of a possibility to be exploited, in the sense of what is *indefinitely shareable*, and this is so by and in a common intelligence, thereby producing, through continuous overflowing, a comprehension which goes beyond (will endlessly have to go beyond) every frontier and every particular, doing so by means of integrating them. Only such a communicability in the intelligible, not one that is believed to be given, but that is in process, will keep this commonality [*commun*] open. It is in this power to exist and to develop that the common exists, and not in some prior condition. I *can* learn to appreciate works of art from any age and any tradition, and I can communicate with them. This is the case even when the demands established by their production are unknown or are contrasting (a Renaissance Madonna just as much as a Cubist painting). In the same way, although I have been formed by the grammar of the *logos*, I *can* learn to read texts which defeat the demands it makes, whether they come from ancient China or contemporary poetry.

Could this theoretical act of Apel and Habermas (an act which is, however, as classical and reassuring as could be, that of re-inscribing the requisite into a native constitution, and therefore of once more clinging to the old dogma of human nature) avoid the most obvious traps? These dogmas confront any enterprise which seeks to *ground itself* in the 'originary'; they are ones, consequently, that have to articulate culture with nature. This means that they have to designate a point of possible co-ordination between what would arise *a priori* from an intangible and predetermined law and the mutating course of History. They would be unable to extricate themselves from these risky retro-projections. As Apel says, '. . . These pre-suppositions which are implied in the claim they make to performative validity must in some way have resulted from human evolution, and especially from the history of the human community' (Apel, 1981: 587-8). The formulation itself is enough to reveal his awkward position. Rather than this doubtful and nebulous 'must', which is *reconstructed* and serves in such a fragile way as a throne for Duty to the Rule, I prefer what is born from the exercise and rigorous *power* of the faculties alone – whose development from that point on can now be recognized without any difficulty. Humanity is 'on the march', we say, and so is its intelligence. This means that the common should be considered, as the universal was earlier, not from the angle of the given (that of notions or of prescriptions possessed from the outset) but from what is *underway* or proceeding. This continuously generating power of the *intelligible* follows the example of the *universalizing*. It does so consequently not from the angle of a 'constitutive', as Kant would have it, but once again on a 'regulative' basis, so conducting the search and pushing ever farther the effectiveness of sharing. This therefore means not from the angle of the pre-condition (pre-supposition), but by way of a never-concluded operation. The common is thus not a state or a skill – it is something always to be conquered and deployed.

Or was it necessary to fall back on this other option? Faced with these conceptions of the common that we discover in turn to be without a way out (that of the synthesis or the denominator or even the foundation), the response has often been a shrug of the shoulders, and via the opposite direction from any intellectualism to avoid getting involved with these difficulties. Do you not therefore see that this commonality [*commun*] of humanity is simply that of the *lived*? We observe it in *experience*. It is in fact true that, when I read the ancient Chinese (or the ancient Greeks), and do so in such a way as to apply myself to following the various forks their thinking takes, then I do not, for all that, have to presume that something in our experiences differs, since experience itself continuously overflows what thought has taken from it, set and measured. Proof of this is what poetry, by remaining closer to its level, gives access to (Hector and Andromache on the walls of Troy or the nostalgic laments of ancient China). Who would not feel (or would deny) that these themes are immediately shareable (lyricism's well-known 'invariants')? Will this lead me to conclude, however, that 'experience' is always common? On the other hand, what do I share of the feeling of shame Homer's heroes equally display, or of their fear of madness emanating from the gods, the *até*? I *can* nonetheless communicate with them, as I can communicate with the totemism of some and the animism of others by walking through the museum of primal art. At least I can if I make the effort to enter into these singular logics in such a way that, even if there is still a lot of the human that remains alien to me, to turn Terence's formula the other way round, I *can* nonetheless still understand it.

If, therefore, experience being precisely too 'empirical' and variable to make a foundation for the common, I choose to situate this common, between cultures, on the plane of the *intelligible*, this holds for both: on the one hand, because what is shared, from one culture to another, is less of the order of some common ground, according to that imagination resting on something originary, than this very communicability, *Mitteilbarkeit*. And, on the other hand, because this common is what is constantly deployed by 'intelligence', as a faculty of opening, which I also understand, following the example of the *universalizing*, in an active sense, in the gerundive, this *intelligent* ('intelligibilizing') component consisting in being able to circulate between various intelligibilities so that in each case a *coherence* springs forth. For if 'truth' is marked too much by the choice of philosophy, or if even 'reason' still remains too much under the seal of the history of European thought alone, I believe that in the end *coherence* is the correct term and it is one which forms a bridge (see the *li* in Chinese). What I discover in thought from elsewhere or from here is still 'co-herent', since it is effectively held together and internally justified. Thus *intelligence* is really that common resource, always in development as well as infinitely shareable, for the apprehension of coherences and the process of communication through them. We may recall that Heraclitus long ago said: 'Thought is common to all', *phronein*. This makes me set down as a principle the fact that there is nothing, in any culture whatsoever, which would not be intelligible in principle. Such is really, once again, the only transcendental I might recognize, not in terms of given categories, in the name of a preformed reason, but as an exigency forming a never-ending horizon (and responding in this way to the universal). It therefore leaves no residue. And in an absolute way. Even if the efforts of anthropologists are never completely concluded, even if I am never myself certain of being sufficiently successful at reading . . .

XII On 'Cultures': divergences of language – the resources of thought

1 To pose the *intelligibility of cultures* in principle (not only theoretically but also ethically and politically) raises at least two questions. This is so on both sides of the notion and composing it. For, in the first place, why simply be satisfied with the intelligible alone? 'Why, in fact', people ask me, 'don't you start with values when conceiving the relation of cultures? You have not yet started to speak about them . . .' The response is simple: the old alternative of the material and the formal would be revealed as being disappointing here as elsewhere. This is because, on the formal side, there is always the risk that the formalization proposed remains dependent on a particular it does not suspect: proof of this was shown by what we just considered about the communicational pre-conditions invoked by Apel and Habermas. On the other side, envisaging cultures from the 'material' angle, that of content and values, would necessarily result in a balance of power between cultures – for, as soon as value systems cease to correspond, their *options* tend to be mutually exclusive (after Nietzsche there is hardly any mystery about this) and the result is an open or latent war. Either I impose my values on others, or I give in to them; either I affirm my power by exporting *my* universality, or I show (through weakness) my 'goodwill'.

But couldn't people negotiate? The trouble is that I believe it is clear that values *are not negotiable*. Between cultures peace does not arrive by dulling their edges, by reducing their range – in other words, by each of them falling back to their own side; or if it did, it would be a deleterious or simulated peace. The solution, in other words, lies not in *compromise*, but in *comprehension*. Tolerance towards different cultural values, whose urgency is continually being expressed between nations today, should not come (it must not do so simply because it cannot) from each party, whether a person or a civilization, reducing the claims of its own values or by moderating its commitment to them, or even by 'relativizing' its positions (why would Europe haggle to even the slightest degree about Freedom?), that is to say by treating them as less important values whose absoluteness and ideality could be sacrificed – each making an effort and smoothing out its conceptions while giving ground and 'watering down its wine', as is expressed in such a despicably familiar way by 'good sense', which is the opposite of *common sense*. But doesn't the thing still exist, even if in a low and familiar way, of the order of minor considerations, and in an indelible way?

Such tolerance can come only from shared intelligence, from the way that each culture and each person renders the values of the other intelligible in their own language and, consequently, becomes able to reflect upon the basis they have established. This also makes it possible to *work with them*. Or if what is necessary, in this realm still more than others, is what is customarily called 'wisdom', and therefore some form of 'happy medium', here again I believe (I consider this to be a more stimulating version of Confucianism; see Jullien, 1998: 15) that this cannot be understood in a lazy way, as a medium term, or halfway or midway point. It cannot consist in each of the parties compromising, each taking a step back, in a spirit of concession, by seeking conciliation so as to avoid excesses, but only in each of them equally being open, through intelligence, to the conceptions of the other. The aptness of the medium [*milieu*] lies in this 'equal' of the equal opening up. Or, to express it differently again, this 'medium' [*milieu*] of tolerance is not one of disengagement, but of an *opening out*, being finally instigated on both sides intelligently as something face-to-face made from the various possibilities engaged in by thought. For, let us say it again to forestall this fallacious option, wisdom, even that 'of nations', will in no way be found in renunciation – even if this would only be a matter of accommodations. It is obvious that this would sink us into an extraordinarily resigned, dispassionate, consensual, and at same the time boring, conception of culture.

The other examination relates to the plural: is this 'of' (of cultures) pertinent? Doesn't it tend to break down fallaciously into separated entities (as though they were actual beings or even essences) what is manifested in reality as a continuous flux, that is brewing and mingling, hybridizing and mutating ceaselessly, and is therefore lacking a secured determination? But to be precise: a mingling *from what*, if it is not always from a plurality? This leads us to think that culture cannot exist only in the singular, and that the plural, far from simply opening up a variation, is in fact an integral part of it. For if it is true that we continually see

cultures borrow, assimilate, blend into vaster wholes, efface their spe-
cificities and, finally, standardize themselves, we also continually observe
the opposite movement at the same time: continuous re-specification and
re-individuation. Just as they constantly globalize themselves so they
are also being reconstituted in a local way, for culture is always a matter
of a home, of an 'environment' [*milieu*] as Nietzsche said; it is properly
eco-logical. Even the cultural transformations in globalization's regime
show this: while cultural differences and 'exceptions' between countries
as between continents (those which are recognized and partly cata-
logued) are glossed over, or become folklore, or are placed in museums,
or get transformed into clichés, into other cultural communities, indeed
counter-cultural ones, or are divided up differently (into those of work, of
the suburbs, linked to modes of sexuality, on the Internet and so on), but
they still reconstitute themselves from beneath the surface (*underground*).

It then becomes a question, in this doubly contradictory and alternative movement (as we customarily speak of an 'alternative culture'), of
the very essence of the cultural. Culture is always in a process at once of
homogenizing and heterogenizing itself, of confounding and demarcat-
ing, of dis-identifying and re-identifying, of conforming and resisting,
of imposing (dominating) and entering into dissidence. The two are
inseparable: an extension to the point of the abrogation of limits on the
one hand and the work of negativity on the other. If the cultural does not
thereby, under this tension, stop transforming itself, if this is its essence
(the Chinese language admirably says it in its own way, as *wen-hua*,
'culture-transformation'), it is because culture is essentially a phenomenon of alteration (and when I see my listeners or readers transforming
what I say, interpreting it in terms of their own habits and references, I
find that this too is legitimate). The plurality of cultures is therefore not
only not to be understood in a secondary way, as that which would make
cultures just so many modulations or even specifications of a unitary
phenomenon. The issue is even greater: a culture which would become
the culture, in the singular, whether we are speaking of one country or the
whole world, is already a dead culture.

From this plurality of cultures there still flow at least two questions
– in fact, isn't it time to remove 'culture' from hollow, journalistic or
ministerial phrases, which drown the notion in this swamp, between the

great wheels of Leisure and Communication, and make it very boring: how can we still endure them? In fact, if culture is understood, inseparably, in the plural as in the singular (since culture always exists only as diverse cultures, just as it is always at once personal and collective), what is the relation of the cultural subject to his culture? What does the term 'my culture' mean and how can I express it? Expressing it first of all negatively by these two equally naive ends, would be to acknowledge that the cultural subject is neither passive nor possessive. The cultural subject is not passive: I really belong to a cultural whole or to a collective (of language, history, religious tradition, generation and so on) as I also speak of 'my' family, but it is a belonging-dependency that I cannot be content to undergo as an 'atavism', *eine Art von Atavismus* (Nietzsche, 1966: § 20, 217). It is one that I can (must) work with, in other words that I am called upon to *transform*, since this is equally what is proper to culture. Such is even, as far as I am concerned, the primary ethical exigency, which comes even before any choice and determination of my morality: a subject constitutes himself only in so far as he has known how (dared) to take a step back in his mind, to reconsider the buried and sedimented prejudice from which he thinks and, hence, to rediscover an initiative in his thinking. This is a way, of course, of renewing the rending that is the characteristic of philosophy, but by going back to this side of the familiar 'doubt' that is traditionally its threshold. Since, in taking the diversity of languages and cultures into account from that point on, I carry over the suspicion, from the objects of my thought (those Cartesian objects which form the classical setting of philosophy: perception, mathematics, God, the soul, the will and so on) onto the *implicit elements* that produced them.

But neither is this cultural subject any more possessive. When I speak of 'my' culture, I can understand it even less in terms of a property due to the fact that it is most often through the encounter with another culture that one becomes aware of the culture 'from which one comes', in which one has been raised – that's to say, through which a subject is each time awakened. And it is even only by emerging from our own culture that we take into account how much we do not know about the culture we so peremptorily (possessively) consider to be our own. 'The well known in general is unknown precisely because it is *well known*', '*weil es bekannt ist, nicht erkannt*' (Hegel, 1977: § 2). For the known is not the familiar: if we are to apprehend it, don't we even have to start by breaking this addictive familiarity so as to place ourselves in a position by which we might attain it? For my part, I have been able to characterize a little more closely what constitutes 'Europe' only by going 'to China', as it turned me back towards 'my' culture. This even constitutes what I see as one of the main aspects of my work. This is to effect the emergence of the implicit and largely buried choices which have formed Europe and are assimilated by it as if they were self-evident by considering those Chinese perspectives that have been constituted alongside them (this can be applied in respect of modelling, the theoretical, the ideal, the Nude, the *agôn*, dialogue and so on). Before I had begun to read Plato or Aristotle *from the outside*, by using Chinese thinkers as the starting point, I had read them through what they said, constructed, refuted and argued, but not in what they conveyed as self-evident, because it was articulated in the Greek language and *ethos*, which due to this very fact they did not question. Indeed, it was what they did not dream of questioning; what they did not conceive of thinking about.

There is even more to it than this. A culture does not possess itself as one might possess something *in addition* (in addition to nature or what is vital); it is not a supplementary, pellicular masking, something added to the transcendental subject. The cultural is neither isolatable (as a particular sector of activity), nor is it stabilizable (since it is continually transforming itself), and nor is it detachable (from the subjects concerned). Or, if culture is traditionally considered to be something acquired, it has to be recognized that this acquisition goes back to the very origin. I express myself, conceive and work only in a cultural way (the 'nature'/'culture' divide forms in itself an ossified antagonism that is today widely seen as something to go beyond – see also the work of Philippe Descola or Jean-Marie Schaeffer). If I spoke earlier of the *cultural subject*, it is because I therefore consider the cultural existence of the subject as existing prior to its classical determinations as constructed by philosophy, but which it believes universally form a point of departure (like those of the subject of 'knowledge' or the subject of 'action', as an epistemological or moral subject).

From China we can even see more clearly how many questions (like the ones Kant thought he was able to pose, in assuming that the subject is universal – according to those categories whose cultural dependency it did not occur to him to suspect: 'What can I know?' 'What should I do?' 'What do I have the right to hope for?') are still trapped, in spite of their abstraction, in implicit civilizational choices (like the isolation of a plane of pure 'knowledge' or morality as an imperative or the – divine – Promise and the expectation, and so on). Even if the confession might initially appear to be disappointing, let us recognize that we never *pose primary questions*, as we perhaps still naively believe we do, unless they are *folded* into the cultural. 'To fold', as the French familiarly say, is already *to tidy up*. These questions close off (other possibilities) at the same time as they open up. This applies even to those questions we would believe to be most general ('What is man?' or 'Does God exist?'), Greek questions *par excellence* that I have never seen raised in China and which need an infinite number of singular questions to construct and isolate. This leads to the thought that, following the example and in the continuance of language, and, like it, at the same time a received legacy, a medium and a potential to be exploited, the (a) culture is really that *through which* a subject exists; it is the dimension of deployment and effectivization of the subject (or, expressed inversely, and by way of consequence, the subject which does not develop culturally is, as we observe every day, an atrophied subject).

But the other question then posed by this plurality of cultures puts even their study in peril. For as they themselves offer no outline, since they are endlessly transforming themselves, the possibility of characterizing them becomes, to say the least, hypothetical. Every culture, and above all the culture of Europe, is forever altering itself and mutating, de-specifying itself so as to re-specify itself in different ways. What features are therefore to be retained which would not be a caricature or a cliché of it? What is more stereotyped, indeed more fastidiously dwelt upon, than what is said about European 'dualism' or what is organised under the label of the 'Cartesian', or under that fallacious partnership of the 'Judeo-Christian', and so on? How can we even fail to notice that the so-called dominant features of a culture, those we consider most manifest, are frequently also the least interesting? Are they therefore still pertinent? More discreet features are more significant, for what is most emphasized is not what is most operative; and those aspects which are treated as being most outstanding always run the risk of the counter-example and are contested through these exceptions.

This is why I have chosen to distinguish from these dominant features what I call, inspired by Taoist principles ('In every discussion, there is the undiscussed', says the *Zhuangzi* – in this respect see Jullien, 2006: 158), the *ground of understanding* by which one culture, even without ceasing to diversify, no less continues to communicate with itself and to 'understand' itself, to maintain an internal intelligence across its altera-tions and dissensions. Just as there is what is 'undiscussed' – in other words, what does not emerge in the discussion – from which alone we can discuss and even oppose each other (this 'we' already forming a community), for without it we would be unable to begin by meeting each other – there is a *ground of cultural understanding*, on the broadest scale but one that is equally implicit, from which alone culture and thought can be challenged, opposed and transformed. This ground of understanding, as a condition of possibility for these divergences and mutations, is more productive than the most emphasized features, but it is no less coherent; or rather it interweaves what I call a *connivance* between the subjects of the cultural community. It is within it, transported internally as evidence, that the Western sinologist thereby little by little, patiently and from the outside, enters, by acquiring what I earlier called a 'skill'. Equally, by travelling between China and Europe, it has been this ground of understanding, and not schematic features, abstracted from their context and de-historicized, that I have sought to reveal in my work, through a reflection of one upon the other and from both sides.

2 The 'divergence' I have just evoked is not difference – what difference is there between them? It is not only that difference is understood from the point of view of *distinction*, and divergence from the point of view of *distance*: the first from an aspectual angle, the second from that of separa-tion. Or rather, bearing this in mind, something that especially deserves to be recalled is that divergence aims not simply at the objectives of anal-ysis but, by the distance opened up, *sets in tension* what it has separated. While difference is opposed to the same and to the identical, and serves as a descriptive category (as the Platonic differentiation of essences, the *diairesis tôn eidôn*, already did), divergence for its part opposes the

expected, the ordinary and the predictable, or at least it reveals another possibility. Its point of view infringes, even if in an implicit way, upon the normative; the divergence it operates is not reduced to a diversification. Or, to express it differently again, differently from difference being understood in this perspective of description, divergence is understood under the angle of exploration: it envisages an elsewhere and explores the extent to which other paths can be cleared. An heuristic advantage is drawn from it, and this is what makes its concept useful to me as I think about the relation of cultures. To speak of the difference of languages, in particular, would be to limit us to developing this plurality by giving an inventory of the multiplicity of structures and forms, while dealing with the divergence of languages leads us to probe *where* these singularities *can go* and what by-ways they open up in thought. In the same way, if I say not that Aristotle's thought on such a point is different from that of Plato, but that it diverges or digresses from it, it is because I want to reveal what, by opening out what is thinkable, is risky about the bifurcation and detachment operated. By doing so the inventive work of thought may be revealed.

The other choice, for me, is precisely to begin by considering this divergence of cultures by starting from language. When I speak of 'Chinese thought', I am not assuming that it contains some particular essence according to which it can be distinguished, but I am simply designating the thought which has been expressed in Chinese (and in the same way, 'Greek thought' is that which is expressed in Greek). But the *divergence* we then notice between these languages effectively opens other possibilities for thought. I return to this elementary experience which I have often cited (see Jullien, 2000: 59, 'The first lesson in Chinese'): in order to express 'thing' (the first word learned in the first lesson), the Chinese say 'east-west' (*dong-xi*; to express 'What is this thing?' they say 'What is this east-west?'). Although when I was a young Hellenist I still questioned myself about the usefulness, as an apprentice philosopher, of committing myself to the study of a new language, and one reputed to be so difficult, I found that it provided an initial confirmation. Could I even say, verging on an oxymoron, that it was a theoretical 'revelation'? It was all the more noticeable, moreover, in that, as is ordinarily the case when something happens which we consider worthy of being called a 'revelation', the other people around us seem to continue impassively on their way. It occurs without their having been troubled – without their even noticing what has struck us so forcefully . . .

To express 'thing', a word which for us is the most primary as well as the most unitary and elementary one, one that is at once so compact and the least fissurable, inheriting from *causa* the interest for the matter at issue at the same time as conveying, from *res*, the meaning of matter, substance and property, the Chinese thus express a relation of opposites. In order to grasp what continually rises up before us as something with which to be concerned, they express the interaction between the poles within which reality is constantly occurring, and at which it aims (but here I am still trapped in *res* as I try to express it). More than a simple difference, there is really in this a *divergence* which clears another path, diverging from our most embedded notional expectations, one whose incidence we will then never stop measuring. And above all it opens up another conception of the 'real', not from the angle of Being or 'thing-ness' but as continuous exchange and communication between the factors, *yin* and *yang*, from which this incessant process flows, and so on.

> In truth such a divergence and *unfolding*, as offered by the diversity of languages, makes for no more than a beginning. For how is 'landscape' expressed in Chinese? (See Jullien, 2003: ch. 9, 'The spirit of a landscape'). Not as the great European languages express it from a perceptive and definitive experience, in unison and barely questioning themselves about their choice (compare *Landscape*, *Land-schaft*, or *paesetto*, *paesaggio*, and so on), as that part of the land which nature presents to the eyes of those who gaze on it and which extends as far as the view can extend it; in other words as the aspect of this 'land' (*pagus*) such as it allows itself to be embraced by whoever contemplates it and that, across the expanse, is carved up by vision. To express 'landscape', the Chinese (even modern Chinese) say 'mountain(s)-water(s)' (*shan-shui*) or 'mountain(s)-river(s)' (*shan-chuan*). Once again, the point of view expressed in language is not that of an aspectual identification and demarcation, but of the interaction between poles: those of High and Low, or vertical and horizontal, of compact (bulk: the mountain) and fluid (the ungraspable: water). Or of the opaque and the transparent, the fixed (the mountain,

the proverb says, 'does not move') and the mobile, and so on. 'Mountain(s)-water(s)' symbolizes so many complementary oppositions, stretching the world, and the infinite exchanges which result from them. Thus, far from allowing itself to be conceived as a portion or fraction of land submitted to the authority of the gaze and demarcated by a horizon, the Chinese 'landscape' puts to work the functional global nature of elements, or rather of factors (vectors) in interaction. It is enough to consider the classical paintings of Europe and China in order to measure this: Chinese painting does not paint a corner of the world from the position of a perceptive subject and in such a way as he would construct it through perspective. Instead it is the totality of cosmic dynamism and breath, such as they are deployed in the great proceedings of the world through the infinitely diverse play of its polarities, that the impetus animating the pencil is entrusted with conveying.

From this we return unfailingly to the question which becomes central: transcending these divergences between languages and the inherent divergences which consequently result from them, are there no categories of thought that would be found everywhere and which would necessarily be identical? For it is true that philosophy for its part took pains to draw up the table of such categories, at the same time leading us back towards the conception of universals which would be given to the mind at the outset. In short, they would have come before 'Babel' . . . But it has also been noted often enough, in Benveniste and even before, a century earlier, by F. A. Trendelenburg in Germany, that Aristotle's categories (the first, following the conceptions of genres in the *Sophist*, to undertake such a systematization and tabulation) were in reality only those which might have been suggested to him, or 'prompted', by the Greek language. These were 'essence', 'quantity', 'quality', 'relation' and so on. Through such categories, perceived under the angle of 'what is said' – in other words, of predication and its forms (*ta skhêmata tês ketêgorias*) – the Stagirite thereby only reflected and exploited the principal options, or prejudices, in the capacity his own language articulated so as to express the world.

But what then of Kant who, in *Pure Reason*, presented a table of categories in which it was precisely affirmed that these are not part of language but of the understanding? As concepts, 'stock concepts' that the mind contains *a priori*, as Kant tells us, they tally with logical functions and are deduced from a transcendental point of view (Kant, 1969: I, 2). But is a category like that of 'substance' ('inherence'), for example, which Kant introduces under the relation, actually imprinted with this logical imperative [*devoir-être*], which confers upon it such a pre-established universality? If I consider it by bringing into play the divergence of the Chinese language and thought, I might see in it rather the persistence of the Greek ontological point of view and its representation, especially in Aristotle, of 'what remains below' (all the casual changes, as *hupokeimenon*): 'sub-ject', 'sub-stratum', 'sub-stance', in short this 'essential' *support* of all determinations, which does not itself relate to anything else, but to which everything else is related, and it does this by means of 'accident'. What is therefore contained ('inherent') in this are diverse properties and qualities. However far the effort of abstraction might have been impelled, Kant thus remained within the fold that linked logic to the ontological and to being founded on the attributive relation of predication, the point of view precisely of the *thing* ('substance') which happens, *in addition*, to be this one or that one. But, once again, the Chinese, who have left the predicative link a lot looser, have not isolated a concept of 'matter' (the cosmic prompting, *qi*, is neither matter nor mind, or it is both at once). They have not developed a notion of essence, nor have they thought from the angle of the 'what is it?'. Their thinking has taken the form of interaction and processive flux. Due to this, the Chinese highlight from without what is still singular about the Western choice of the one rather than the other, which, thanks to the proven success of the science that has been built upon it, is today spread uniformly the world over.

> I admit we need a lot of audacity if we are to dare to bring the list of Kantian categories established as a logical table into question . . . In order to subject them to review, I will continue my examination with examples from China. Is 'causality', for example, central to ways of thinking in China? There is a well-established notion of it (*gu*), which is especially dear to the Mohists, but thinking in China has been articulated rather more under the angle of internal *implication* and deployment, following a relation

of condition to consequence. Evidence for this is the fact that in China there has been no development of any sort of Newtonian causalist physics, something upon which Kant relies. In the same way, does it have any conception of 'community' as a 'reciprocal action between agent and patient'? Since in Chinese the opposition between passive and active voices of conjugation has not been morphologically established, and since it has not semantically developed that between 'suffering' and 'acting' (*paskhein/poiein*: these were already Aristotle's last categories), Chinese thought has conceived community through the diffuse spread of encouragement (the notion of *gan-tong*). It is thus particularly suited to grasping what it is (but this 'what' is already too substantialist) that influences, crosses, continually passes and animates and which is neither subject nor object and neither active nor passive. Another example: is the 'existence—non-existence' opposition entirely relevant to it, even if we are aware that the 'there is not' of the Taoists, which is the 'mother', means the 'there is not' (of actuality, *wu*) – not non-being, but the Undifferentiated? (And what verb is there in classical Chinese to express 'to exist'? *Cun* means 'to subsist'.) Or what is presented in it by the 'necessity – contingency' opposition that is inescapably constraining, when Chinese language-thinking excels in expressing the *opportune encounter*? Under many aspects, as soon as we look a little closer, we see that Chinese language-thought has a *side-ways* approach to such categories – I will come back to this term. To approach 'side-ways' means to be tangential to their demands and not to get bogged down in them. It does not consider them to be false, properly speaking, but rather that application of categories would render it sterile.

3 It appears to me that the point of view, or the watchword to be retained, therefore has to be this in the relation we maintain with the plurality of cultures: to combat, as I have just said, their *sterilization*; or, seen positively, to favour their fertility. This is precisely what the thought of divergence would achieve if it were to be detached from the *topos* of difference with which I started so as to thwart the reign of the uniform. There is a further step to take. Divergence being the angle from which other possibilities are explored and deployed, the everlasting question of

the same and the identical stands out for us all at once and in a salutary way. I will not defend *cultural identity* (including that in France), to which the point of view of difference traditionally leads us, since the very essence of culture is to mutate and to change: this demand for identity is an impossible stiffening which cannot be maintained except by means of external arguments and positions (and above all by political ones such as nationalism). Instead, I will call for a struggle against the *loss*, through globalized sterilization, of the cultural forms and coherences of thought which could contribute to the development (not in a museum but into the future) of the cultural and the thinkable (the theme of – French – cultural 'exception' clumsily expresses this in its way). But the concept of divergence is a rigorous and combative concept in this respect: by leading us to probe *the point to which* divergences could lead, to measure the distance which opens up between them, it *unfolds* the cultural and the thinkable to their limit; but also, in an inverse sense, taking us back, due to this offer of dispersion, into their implicit choices at the beginning of their separation and right back to the logic of what one will really be led consequently to figure, on either side, on the basis of equality and even as so many alternatives for thought.

The point of view of the *divergence* thereby awakens the cultural and the thinkable from their drowsy normativity. No longer considering them flatly, under the angle of difference, but *in tension* and under the angle of dissidence, leading them to consideration, in this 'point to which' (the point to which the path cleared can go – can lead – from both sides), under the angle of their potentiality. It thereby substitutes the point of view of exploration – exploitation for that of identification (of difference), since divergence opens up possibilities. These divergences, and above all those that have been noted in language, are to be considered as so many *resources* for thought. Do we ourselves, at a time of standardized covering-over, not have to become 'diviners' of culture? Isn't our task to bring its buried deposits back to the surface as we follow their fertile and forsaken veins (furrows)? Now that we are finally concerned at the planetary level – even if it is a bit late – about natural resources which we fear may be drying up, why should we not *also* be concerned about these cultural resources, which we see being sterilized under globalized normativity and becoming more and more hidden or, worse, travestied?

We would do this not so as to alter, as is the essence of culture, but rather to deform and *play at* (at being culturally 'authentic'). What is worse (and more false) today than the spectacles described as traditional, and the local entertainments displaying the pseudo-singular (these 'entertainments' being the exact opposite of festivities, and so on)?

Let us then conversely measure the consequences from the actual point of view of philosophy. This is where account can finally be taken of the divergences between languages, and therefore also between the thoughts which have unfolded from them (as I said earlier, primary questions are never posed but are always *folded* into language), allowing us to emerge (forcing us to emerge) from the reference to truth which until now has obsessed thought so much, at least in Europe. By taking its distance from the normative, in other words by substituting an exploratory point of view for it and probing the resource, inviting consideration of the cultural and the thinkable in terms of cleared paths, and therefore also of equally possible choices, divergence liberates from the exclusivity of the true rejecting the false. One culture, and therefore the thought which has developed in it, is no more true than any other: Chinese culture-thought is no more – or less – true than the European is. But a culture (a thought), according to the possibilities it exploits, is more or less fertile; according to the veins followed, it may go more or less far in one direction or another. A culture or a thought is therefore not measured in terms of truth, but in those of development and *yield*: the totemism or animism anthropologists describe for us are no more false than any other 'conceptions of the world', but their mastery of the 'objective' world, according to the European category, has lesser effect. Inversely, in having detached 'nature' from a self-subject and constituted it as a knowable object, European 'naturalism' (I am borrowing this term from Philippe Descola, 2005) has discovered an unheard-of operativity, one which pulls it violently out of phase with other cultures and precipitates humanity onto a new course.

I immediately hear the objection and make the point more precisely: this does not for all that mean relativizing truth (that is, returning to sceptical discourse), but inviting it to retreat from its global imperialism and *localizing* it – putting it back in its proper place. Its particular pertinence (but one which as such is absolute) is that of the invention of science and the discourse of knowledge (with which philosophy and, in its wake, theology – thereby dogmatically losing the sense of the religious – have been, it is true, in great part merged). Or, to express this in a different way: it is to designate as the negative of thought not what is false, which moreover we know works dialectically in so many ways with the true, but the *unthought*. A language, a culture or a thought, in its divergence, furnishes other engagements with (another glimpse of) the *unthought*. And its fecundity is measured by the power of this engagement and this glimpse.

This is thus what we see occurring between China and Greece, whose *divergences of thought* I have tried in my work to reconstruct and to operate upon so as to *place them in tension* with one another by envisaging their respective productivity in the deployment of the thinkable, but not, properly speaking, so as to compare them (in other words, under the insufficiently fertile angle of difference). In turning to account the resources of the verb *To Be* (grounding in a single sense the uses of predication and identity), in giving full rein to the representation of separation (*chôrismos*: between the sensible/intelligible, concrete/abstract, becoming/eternal, and so on), by impelling exploration by causality as far as it is possible to take it (in which everything is explained by cause, and God himself 'is cause'), but above all by making good use of its syntactical rules and functions, Greek language – culture – thought is essentially *constructive* (of essences, transcendence, finality, paradigms and so on). This is not the determinism of language, but rather the *deployment* of its 'pre-dispositions' (Benveniste, 1971).[1] At a global level, the ontological point of view furnishes an 'engagement', a term I will return to, whose explicative capacity carried classical science along. But what other engagements are revealed, or what other efforts are authorized, by a type of thinking which would have developed not according to these prejudices, but by *passing alongside them*?

What follows is this: because its language neither declines nor conjugates, because it is not constrained to decide between genders, between tenses, between modes and not even between the plural and the singular, because it has not formalized the predicative relation (neither necessarily giving the verb an explicit subject, nor categorically assigning modalities linked to a subject, or the 'thus' to a *this*; see the *Zhuangzi*) and because it is almost without syntax (at least in classical Chinese: 'empty' words link 'full' words in it, introducing play and breathing space between them), China is more fitted to express (to think) not essence and determination, but flux, the 'between', the impersonal, the continuous, the transitional – interaction and transformation (at least according to the terms we possess). I have not said that it is unaware of transcendence but that, in this way, it is lacking in comparison to the sublimity of European constructions. Concerning what we designate as 'immanence', on the other hand, and on which European thought is unable to construct (immanence precisely does not construct itself), it is astonishingly at ease when evoking it – each 'thus' being no longer ascribed to some substance – substratum – subject, but being understood *sufficiently* in its procedural course alone – such is the plenitude of the 'way', *tao* (see Jullien, 2006: ch. 12).

> For example, let's return to thinking about what we call 'time'. We ('we': in Europe) have caught the present in pincers by separating it morphologically at once from the past and from the future, and we have done so to the point of rendering its extension inconceivable (this 'present' is divided endlessly between the parts of the future and the past) and therefore of doubting its existence – which is not without consequences for thinking about 'living' (see Jullien, 2001: chs. 1-4). Moreover, Montaigne adroitly did not speak of living in the present, but 'in a timely way' . . . Caught in the trap of conjugation and in the impasse of its distinctions, we have therefore been unable to develop thinking about 'time' other than by reference to space (which is what philosophy since then has not failed to criticize), and more precisely to questions of place: 'from', 'towards', 'where it is going'. 'From what is not yet, through what is without extension, it [time] runs towards what is no more', said Augustine (1962: XI, 21). Augustine had no other *resource* by which to think about time than to deploy questions of place in Latin: *unde, qua, quo*. There remains the fourth case available, the place where one is, *ubi*, which provides him with a convenient means by which (or of which he makes use) to situate Eternity. For the Chinese language not only does not conjugate and therefore does not separate tenses in a decisive way (it occasionally marks the near future and the past), and so does

not distinguish between these questions of place, but also equally thinks about the course of what we call 'time' under the lens not of Being (in this case, no time 'exists': neither the past which no longer 'is', nor the future which 'is' not yet, nor the present which 'is' merely the point of passage from one into the other, which is where the aporia lies) but once again that of polarity. The formula is (I will try to translate it as closely as possible): 'going away: past – present: coming' (*wang gu jin lai*). What we in Europe have sought to identify as time is thereby understood, according to the articulation characteristic of the Chinese language, between the poles of the past and the present, from 'to go' and 'to come' and by exchange between them. It is that which (but this substantial- ist 'that which', let's repeat, is too much) is ceaselessly going / ceaselessly coming. Not in a 'distensional' way (like the *distentio* of Augustine tearing the mind apart between separated times) but rather as a continuous transition.

XIII Constructing the dialogue between cultures to counter the surrounding uniformization; human self-reflection

1 If cultures are always plural, what relation is to be promoted between them so as to manage their divergence and so that one does not have to imagine humanity to be heading towards a single culture (in which consciousness would be lost)? Even better: how can it most effectively be implemented? One word usually comes up, and it does not even appear possible to avoid it, nestled as it is in its prominence: 'dialogue'. But *dialogue* appears to be a desperately weak notion in the way its use is licensed in relation to cultures and their lines of confrontation. In the absence of a demanding concept to orient it, dialogue has a soothing effect beneath its irenicism of good will, which is gossipy in its inexhaustible rhetoric. It is a notion that is also suspect due to what it renounces. Doesn't it hide, behind the display of good feelings, a too hastily agreed dispersion of the thought of the Whole – the renunciation of the idea of producing a fresh global form of truth, an unacknowledged desertion of the absolute; in short, below this apparent and commendable pluralism, isn't there a theoretical disengagement which dare not speak its name? Or, from the point of view of *Realpolitik*, isn't it a new form of inability, on the part of Westerners with their imperialism losing its effectiveness, an inability to maintain a hegemonic or controlling discourse, or even a cohesive discourse, any longer? Or otherwise, perhaps, in a more cunning way, a covert means of passing on their universalism, which we see encountering more and more resistance throughout the world, when we take account of how other powers are gaining in strength, and still continuing *mezza voce* so it becomes acceptable in the way it is heard? What sort of 'dialogue' does it mask? To react to this complacent way of thinking, its contrary, 'shock' (clash), between cultures, has been ventured (Huntington, 1996). Instead of trusting in the simple exchange of words with which to calm human relations, this plurality of cultures is designated as a new (and principal) source of conflicts in the world to come.

Huntington's thesis can be summed up in two points. First, of growing and even determining importance, cultural factors in the post-Cold War world: the ideological, political and even economic stakes characterizing that time have given way, and the paradigm to come is civilizational. It then follows that the principal confrontations will henceforth be played out on the cultural level, even between nation-states. And they will come especially from non-Western civilizations re-affirming the value of their own culture, while 'the West's universalist pretensions increasingly bring it into conflict with other civilizations, most seriously with Islam and China' (Huntington, 1996: 20). Against the Fukuyamist thesis of an end to programmed history that arose after the fall of the Berlin Wall, which would be harmonious (but boring) because it was 'the end point of mankind's ideological evolution and the universalization of Western liberal democracy' (Francis Fukuyama quoted by Huntington, 1996: 31), it is easy to show that, for all that, liberal democracy has not triumphed since then and that the war of ideas has not been concluded. It is those civilizations which have attained their full maturity, and are therefore already in decline – such as the Western one – which believe they see eternity finally coming. The scene of conflict has simply changed its appearance and 'dangerous shocks' will be born in the future from the interaction between 'Western arrogance', 'Islamic intolerance' and the 'affirmation of the Chinese self'.

An alarmist (realist) vision thrown down as a challenge to the much-touted globalized cultural co-operation, this nevertheless calls for a response, as far as I am concerned, on two counts. 1. Huntington's attachment to the notion of 'cultural identity' founded on difference, which is therefore to be defended by the community concerned and consequently constituting an inescapable source of antagonism. He has no idea of the fertility of cultural divergences conceived as resources to exploit, even though we actually see they have continually worked to transmute History. 2. A simplistic conception of cultural determinism leading him, in a reductionist way, to characterize cultures according to their most obdurate features – the most marked and solid (see the standard characteristics of the 'Western world' according to NATO which he maintains as a paradigm (Huntington, 1996:

306)). Why consider, for example, that the principal characteristic of Europe (so significant that, if it were to abandon it, this would result in its destruction) is Christianity? Why couldn't it just as easily be rationalism and atheism? Or rather, doesn't rationalism itself work on both sides? Why, since Europe has constantly enriched itself with both (between Plato and Epicurus), shouldn't we recognize both at once (Europe is Christian *and* atheist) as well as the tension between them? For the one did not develop without the other: they are reciprocally sharpened and promoted (in the same way as are materialism and idealism and so on). Indeed, it is this *tension* which makes Europe (and this critique goes just as much for the unsuccessful – because of what various parties have removed – Preamble of the European Constitution).

Huntington doesn't trace back from one or another of these features judged to be the most prominent, but always chosen more or less arbitrarily, to what I earlier conceived as their *ground of understanding*, to this side of them. However, it is only at the stage of these implicit and theoretical pre-expectations that the connivances appear, even between cultural aspects which could seem very distant from, and even contradictory to, one another, thereby giving a glimpse of their form of coherence and backing – this very ground of understanding allowing itself to be better perceived from outside of this culture, as I have said, in an oblique way (as in reconsidering classical Europe from the perspective of China: what *connivance* linked together the Logos – Being – God – Freedom – Finality, and so on). With such rudimentary instruments of analysis, Huntington cannot arrive, for his part, at anything other than purely defensive and, consequently, reactionary conclusions (especially against multiculturalism in the United States, which is his target): there will be salvation for the West only in the unalloyed reaffirmation of its 'traditional values' and its 'identity', judged no longer as 'universal' (this false ideal needing to be abandoned as dangerous) but as *unique* ('. . . to preserve, protect and renew the unique qualities of Western civilisation' (Huntington, 1996: 311).

What other path is there – between, on the one hand, the slack consensus of dialogue still suspected of being an alibi or of burying power struggles more insidiously beneath its apparent opening out and, on the other hand, the clash announced (observed) as well as the appeal to the identitarian fold of the 'West' – which doesn't tip over towards either side and would be neither utopian nor defensive nor compromised? Or rather should 'dia-logue' be reclaimed and reconsidered, but this time by deciding to impose all of its demands on each of its components – something which would allow me at the same time to renew my two earlier propositions and conjoin them? We would do this, on the one hand, by emphasizing the distance of the *divergence* in the *dia* of dia-logue, between necessarily plural cultures, maintaining in tension what is separated, because a dialogue, as the Greeks have taught us, is even more rigorous and fertile when it grapples with antagonistic theses (see Jullien, 2006: the chapter on 'Dia-logue'). And on the other hand, in *logos*, we would see the fact that all cultures together maintain a provisional com-municability and that everything, concerning the cultural, is *intelligible*, without loss or residue. The mere fact that dialogue has never been as egalitarian and neutral as has been sanctimoniously claimed, as it remains prejudiced by power relations and oblique strategies (as Socrates already attested in Plato, his master builder in the West), does not prevent it from being operative *of itself* (or in spite of us). But operative in what way? Not that one would want to find accord with the other at any price, or that one would find formal rules already prescribed within it, but simply because, in order to have a dialogue, each participant must of necessity disclose their position, put it in tension and establish it in relation to something. This doesn't therefore mean that each would be carried along by a finality of understanding, or that the logic of dialogue might reveal a pre-established universal. However, because all dialogue is an efficient (operating) structure which, to enable communication and therefore also gain a focus, *de facto* compels a revision of its own conceptions.

But in what language should the dialogue take place, if it is *between cultures*? Suppose this forms a very thin triangle. Suppose culture is approached first of all from language (rather than from the religion, ideology and so on) and that language is already thought. I will answer, without fear of paradox: each should do so in his language, but by *translating* the other. For translation is the exemplary engagement with the work of operativity that is inherent to dialogue. In fact it forces us to *re-elaborate* at the very heart of our own language. This also means re-considering its implicit aspects, so as to render them available to the eventuality of another meaning, or at least to be taken into other ramifications. Far from being a handicap, as an obstacle and source of opacity – the punishment of Babel – it is the necessity to translate which puts cultures mutually to work. I consider translation to be the only possible ethic of the 'global' world to come. For if communication is made in the language of one of its interlocutors, or without the other language being heard at the same time, the encounter is by this very fact distorted, as it operates on the terrain (and therefore in the play of culturally implicit aspects) of one of the two: the dice are loaded. If this develops in a third language, for example standardized American, the implicit aspects of this language would then pre-orient the exchange, and this is so even in its theoretical organization (by inserting its topics, issues and so on). Under the pretext of contributing its mediation, it interposes itself. This is why I have little faith in the virtues of the 'polylogue' and world culture events organized ritually here and there and being renewed from one year to the next, in this hybrid – and, moreover, largely de-anglicized – English which now serves as a *koiné* of Communication. For, from the outset, the bets have been placed: the so-called 'specificity of cultures' will not be developed except according to Western pre-expectations, themselves flattened out and still incredibly poorly considered.

> This is also why I challenge, just as much as the accusation of essentializing culture (producing concepts is not, for all that, the same as disdaining context and complexity – don't we know that already? – but, on the contrary, means clarifying their coherence), that other accusation (of 'binarism') which has been aimed at me, in a more disguised way, concerning the construction of an encounter between China and Europe (a construction 'all the more appealing and satisfying in that it flatters a natural propensity towards symmetry as a narcissistic return to oneself' (Cheng, 2007: 9)[1] – along with other small idiocies of those who prefer not to understand). The fact is rather that, as soon as I translate, I *am in binarity*; and that, if I 'construct' effectively, it is above all to clarify the conditions of possibility of this translation. There is no overarching position for languages any more than there is for cultures: emerging from this tension between the originals and

their target languages – I can only work in-between them – would
immediately lead to a skimming through (in what language?)
and is always just a way (or rather equivalent to an avoidance) of
reinvesting the categories one began with, in this way once more
leading to the old forms of division and to staying at home.

When, for example, this is proposed in order to show an open mind
and render human rights more acceptable to other cultures ('It is a
matter of giving an account of the very pluralism of rights' – Eberhard,
1999: 273), I note that, in spite of its good will, European thought has
still not left home; it has not started to de-categorize and re-think itself:
the (European) notion of right is varied but not in any way disturbed.
It remains pre-imposed as an initial frame at whose heart alone will an
exchange be possible. The one-to-one relationship of the law when faced
with *ritual*, for example, as it has traditionally developed in China, is still
not envisaged. But can I actually enter into a 'pluralistic' conception if
I keep the concept of right as it is and do not re-work it? We should be
equally wary of this sort of neo-Figurism which is often its consequence:
when we seek by good will (or so as not to disturb the fundamentalism
of its thought) equivalents to human rights in other cultures, aren't we
doing what those European missionaries in China used to do when they
devoted themselves to finding the lineaments of the God of Christian
Revelation in the 'Heaven' of the Chinese or in the *Shangdi*? Isn't this
also the case when we take the system of regulation instigated by the
codified procedures of 'remonstrance', which had in view only limiting
the authoritarianism of the Prince, to be a pre-figuration of 'democracy'
in China, in this way projecting Western expectations onto it?

2 This dialogue that takes cultures, including the Western one, back
to a mutual drawing board, in various encounters [*vis-à-vis*] that are
enjoined to multiply, and this above all through translation, is not just the
only *meaningful* way to elude the clash we see engaged today between
civilizations – by 'civilization' I mean here cultures that have been established in a historical world. In order for divergence to work, it needs to
be placed in tension – in other words, given back its legitimate function
as negation. Or, to express it more explicitly still, by once more crack-
ing open the closed universalities by means of its *dia* in order to liberate

within them the exigency of the surpassing which is proper to the universal, this dia-logue is also the only intelligent way (*logos*) of resisting the surrounding uniformization – as well as (should I say it?) everything tiresome about the world to come.

Each age has its own form of resistance, whether it has been open or discreet – let's define our own: *divergence* is the concept of a cultural resistance which is also ethical and political. For, amongst other simulacra, uniformization has produced that of favouring understanding and peace; we believe it is the source of progress, because it suppresses divergences. But here aren't we deceiving ourselves, once more, about its nature? When it does not respond to ends of pure profit, uniformization is bureaucratic far more than it is democratic (through its pseudo-equality), ingested as it is through anonymous measures. The 'standard' does not equal peace, any more than levelling is equality. The evidence for this is very close at hand, before our very eyes, in the uniformization machine that is 'Brussels'. In so far as Europe will only be brought into existence through uniformization and the reduction of divergences, its construction, along these lines, will be sterile, incapable of being mobilized. As an enterprise of forced homogenization, it will leave the necessary heterogenization only with the poorest and least fertile ways out, those of withdrawal into a closed identity and the stubborn refusal of what nevertheless appears in an undeniable way, to be a *common* construction, to be a logic of History.

> And, first and foremost, which language(s) will be spoken in Europe? Can its legislators neglect the task of making this clear? Europe, however, will not be inventive again until it takes into account the fact that a good part of its invention has been due, precisely, to the plurality of its cultural languages. A 'cultivated' man is above all defined in Europe as one who knows several of them (with Greek and Latin in first place), and it is only by continuing always to borrow and reinterpret, from one language to another, that Europe has revitalized and renewed itself – has *invented* itself: the future of Europe therefore lies in the reciprocal reactivation of the great European languages, rather than in making a standard of one language (whether English or some other) that facilitates communication. The proof is what the beginnings of European

philosophy already taught us. We may recognize that the philosophers were in Greece, but philosophy was nonetheless born
in Rome: in the fumbling translations of Lucretius or Cicero. Or,
if we know that philosophy is a 'Greek thing', as has endlessly
been repeated since Hegel, it became fully itself only by freeing
itself from the idiom in which it appeared. Likewise, if to translate
is to think, the opposite is also true, at least in Europe, and it is
even this that in part formed Europe culturally. To think is always
also, in a certain sense, to translate. From the time of the Greeks,
philosophy has had the good fortune to be a citizen of Babel, and
this has impelled it along.

This proof of translation has not only revealed to philosophy
an exigency of universality, of a trans-linguistic nature, that is
different from what it had conceived by promoting the generality
of the concept – but it has also especially rendered it possible for
thought to seek upstream from itself. Only such groping confrontation with the other language will give philosophy a certain
reflexivity – reflection in the proper sense. It has been able to make
a start at perceiving itself by exporting itself into this other milieu.
By introducing a relative and comparative exteriority of thought
vis-à-vis its language, this confrontation made it recognize and
measure the configuration of the thinkable in which it articulated
itself. In this way it obliquely clarified, through this release from
the idiom, what are at once the implicit and the unwonted aspects
of its thought.

This can be noted even more easily from an external point of
view. We see this capacity for *self-reflection*, which the dispersion
of European languages has conferred upon philosophy, con-
firmed, from China, and by opposition to it. For what above all
distinguishes the Chinese man of letters from the European intellectual, if not the fact that he has only known a single cultural language, as a written language (the language of ideograms alone),
and that this continued up to the end of the nineteenth century?
Even the encounter with Sanskrit, the vehicle for the Buddhist
teachings, hardly changed conditions in China; the translations
of the sutras were made by intermediaries and on its borders. Not
only did the Chinese man of letters not learn another language or
himself confront the difficulty of translation (in other words the

divergence working between languages), but nothing even led him to consider that he was thinking *in language*. This meant that he was deprived of any sideways movement which would allow him to look back into the conditions of his thought. This is no doubt one of the reasons Chinese thought is less philosophically articulated. The Chinese notional semes are endlessly self-reflexive and take 'relish' in themselves but, without the divergence opened up by the disparity of languages, they weren't able to reflect upon or even permit any critical distance in relation to themselves. They offer no opening. They never cease to reel off what is evident (as though they were expressing only a pure immanence) and are not haunted by any anxiety (about their limits or their prejudices). They remain mobile in the allusive networks of their intertextuality, but they are closed to any perspective given by the inter-language. For this reason they barely suspect the comfortableness of their thought – even if this was what created 'wisdom'.

The uniformization that drowns divergences is no more pacifying at the level of the whole world. Soothing it may be, but what contradictions does it resolve? On the contrary, what is repressed is continually at work insidiously accumulating its explosive charge under the layering that uniformization tries to spread over it. In fact has the West even begun to become aware of the *trauma* aroused, in the heart of other cultures, by the obligation they were suddenly forced to meet at the end of the nineteenth century when, faced with the asserted power of Europe, they had to conform to its notional norms and categories, and even above all to its periodization which indexed them in terms of its history alone? The latest avatar of this was given, mounted like a jewel, let us recall, when the 'year 2000' struck . . . For what was the year 2000 once one had departed from the West, even though it was celebrated as a world festivity? In any event, does it mean anything at all in the history of the Arabs, the Hindus or the Chinese? When the Christian missionaries began to disembark in China, in the second half of the sixteenth century, it was noted that their teaching barely touched the Chinese men of letters, most of whom continued to be attached to their own frames of thought: proof, if it was needed, that this external message, both onto- and theological, did not in itself contain anything impressive. On the other hand, when

Europe returned a second time to the 'Far East', no longer with missions but with cannons, and implanted itself by force and through science, the one relying upon the other, the Chinese or Japanese were constrained, in the face of Western supremacy, to open themselves up to European conceptions that were imposed as universal. This meant that the Chinese and Japanese therefore needed to re-confirm their own cultures through a theoretical tool as well as a theoretical exigency that were not their own and whose suitability was for them never even considered – in any case at first. They had to seek a 'philosophy' and even a 'metaphysic', a 'logic', an 'aesthetic'. They had to reconsider their thought according to the carving out of 'subject' and 'object', 'absolute' and 'concrete', 'matter' and 'form', 'being' and 'attribute' and so on. They had to appropriate for themselves our theoretical mythology: of the Beautiful, Truth, Creation and so on.

Today, when we read a text of classical Chinese literature rewritten, in other words re-deployed, into a contemporary Chinese that has itself been re-formatted according to European categories, it offers only the pale reflection of Western cultural expectations. Although written in Chinese, it is a text passed through this categorical uniformization as through a sieve; it is sterilized and disappointing. But under this uniformization absorbing divergence, not only is the meaning, and therefore the possibility for thought, then lost, but also resources are covered over and dried up. But, when faced with this loss, what is also now developing among the Chinese themselves in reaction is the conviction that their culture is incommunicable, that its 'mystery' or its 'essence' is impenetrable to foreigners. In Japan, where the 'Japanese soul', *yamato damashii*, is celebrated, the most summary comparativist discourses about 'Japanese uniqueness' (*nihonjinron*) proliferate. In China the discourse of *Chineseness* is spreading rapidly, demanding a 'cultural nativism' (*bentuzhuyi*), invoking a return to 'native studies', and called upon to differentiate itself from a sinology that is judged to be too Western and lacking 'cultural consanguinity', and even calling for the restoration of the 'circle of sinogrammatical culture' whose basic supposition is that 'the Chinese characters penetrate our thought, our blood, and our collective unconscious' (Wang Yuechuan, quoted in Zhang Yinde's excellent study, 2007: 300). Gaining credence, in this expression of the repressed, is the idea that there is an ineffable quality to culture, which is reinscribed in nature: the cultural *consequently leaves the intelligible*. In other words, it is no longer considered shareable through a common intelligence. The work of dialogue is abandoned. Notions of Chinese 'centrality', or of a 'Chinese mind', or of 'Asiatic values', close up into sectarian, identitarian values, while they believe themselves to be the bearers of an immutable tradition at the same time as having an irreducible originality; and so they unfailingly play the game of nationalist renewal.

3 When it comes down to it, isn't philosophy as reflection, or rather as *resistance*, promoted by working to get beyond the sterility of opposed theses that promotes mental ruts? Not by seeking to negotiate some median position, of compromise, of 'happy medium', between them, so allowing each side to come to terms with one another and reduce any antagonism, but by showing that their antinomy is empty and that the contradiction which is thereby fixed loses hold on another possibility that their blockage prevents from being glimpsed. This fresh initiative does not bring a solution to their conflict, but reconfigures the question in a completely different way; it does not settle the dilemma, but renders it obsolete. The same goes today for those rival theses dividing up opinion, concerning the relation between cultures, and that we see so comfortably installed. On the one side, what I have designated as facile universalism believes, as its supposedly humanist catechism, in notions or values which would be universal from the outset (in those 'words' which we are told are 'encountered in all languages') and whose 'differences appear self-evidently' as so many cultural variations of a preconceived identity (Billeter, 2006: 54, 59, 82; I reply to this in Jullien, 2007: chs. 7 and 11). Against this is the relativist thesis that abandons diverse cultures to their singular perspectives and unique destiny. If one were then to refuse to adhere to the universalist *credo*, which is all the more fiercely defended today because the European culture which has borne it feels its own power to be on the point of faltering, would this necessarily, for all that, mean tipping over into that other undesirable rut of 'culturalism'?[2]

Between these two fixed fantasies of the Same and the Other, of the identitarian withdrawal into the Same and the fascination for the 'great Other', there is in fact something quite different that needs doing. Not, properly speaking, 'between' – let me correct myself, for that would still be to give in to the mirage of the imposed frame – but by diverging equally from them both. Isn't thinking, moreover, always in a certain way *diverging*, by finding another angle on (and engagement with) what is unthought? For today it is not a question for Europe of abandoning the exigencies of its reason, for which the universal is really the keystone holding so many diverse sections of the wall together, but of taking Reason back to the drawing board. I believe this is actually the good fortune of our age, since we are the first generation that globalization has given the opportunity to travel more freely between cultures. That is really, definitively, the opportunity to grasp the flip side of the sterilizing uniformity which it precipitates: that of being able to circulate between various intelligibilities so as to promote a *common* intelligence *through them* – one which certainly has nothing to do with a unique culture. For that to occur it is again necessary to hold two things firmly: at the same time the possible divergence of thoughts *and* the dialogism of the mind. If we no longer trust the inneism of notions which were given in advance (in which Before?) and we liberate ourselves from any definition of 'Man', but without for all that abandoning the commonality [*commun*] of the intelligible, we have here a fresh perspective opening onto thought, calling for the work of a new morning – a 'morning' because it will require fresh forces. I will call this potential construction site *the self-reflecting of the human*. This alone, by the system it establishes, can break with the *self-reflection* that today produces uniformity across the whole planet.

But why speak here of the 'human' and not of 'mankind'? What is it that this withdrawal from the glories substantive of 'Mankind' (with a capital letter) liberates or purges us of? What displacement and loosening up brings it about? That is to say, once again, what possibility is re-opened by putting between parentheses and unlocking what, once more, our mind understands by 'substance' (substrate-subject): of the order of what 'remains below', forming a base, as an implicit sub-strate of the representation and sub-ject (everlastingly) of predication? 'Mankind is . . .' A determination of essence then inevitably follows, imposing its prejudices as a (false) universality. Then what is once again suddenly authorized and comes to light simply through this step to the side, one precisely to the side of the *ad*-jective, the 'human' coming to serve as a substitute for this 'Mankind' henceforth recognised as an old monolith? We recover in this way, in a sideways fashion, what the other term, Mankind, has *sup-posed* too much, precisely in order to be able to intimate that from which this appeal à la Rousseau nevertheless comes back to us: 'Men, be human!' . . .

The inherent property of mankind, its vocation, to put it thus, on the edge of tautology, is to be human. Or, to express it in another way: the 'human' is what expresses mankind's inherent features, what in fact makes its quality appear and be experienced. But is this enough to create a divergence between them? For, from mankind to the human, what is operating is not just a semantic selection and promotion; it is not so much the passage from class to value or from the generic to the ethical which counts here. A revolution in perspectives is operating discreetly. The entire point of view engaged upon is tipped over according to whether one or the other term (mankind or the human) rules the other, and whether the relation of dependency between them is reversed. 'Mankind', as a notion, requires as its due a definition presented in principle, while the 'human' is an openly exploratory concept. I would therefore no longer assume what mankind *is*, but I mark out (explore) what *makes* the human – henceforth with the corollary that it is really the human (its significant, defining features) which *can* form mankind.

What is therefore at once being expressed more and less in the 'human' rather than in 'mankind', and which suffices to open a completely different future for thought? 'Whatever would be the definition given for mankind', said Cicero, 'it is singular and valid for all', *una in omnis valet*. This *hominis definitio*, giving birth to humanism but also enclosing it in a pre-established determination, from that moment on appears pretentious in its subsumption and the way it imposes its universality – at the same time as, by admitting the exchangeable character of its definitional content, it recognizes itself (such is its ambivalence) as strangely hypothetical. A definition, in consequence, that is still verging on the arbitrary: imperious (imperialist) but also artificial. On the other hand, to say that 'I do not consider anything human (*nil humaini*), however distant, as alien to me', taking up Terence's motto (from *The Self Tormentor*, 1988) more literally and once more setting it in motion, makes the human emerge in a radical way from any essentialist, overarching and defining perspective, and conceives it in a prospective and no longer restricted relationship (of tension, implication and non-indifference) which, deployed once again through the negative, on the contrary maintains such a universal as open.

Passing from mankind to the human is not therefore sinking into relativism (itself inevitably still dependent on a generic conception of mankind even if it takes the contrary path) but, by unfolding a never-ending plural, that of multiple cultures as the outstanding features of humanity, it engages us in a work which has no support apart from itself and must always justify its pertinence from within itself alone. What do I have to fear from what I see today of the bigger picture, if I go back into the history of Evolution – that the *hominien* appeared from a progressive *divergence* from other species, themselves slowly issuing from so many earlier divergences, the fish having first taken a step on land and so on? There is no disenchantment here, but rather something to be amazed at if the deployment of life on Earth, through such mutation, has now produced such consciousness and reflexivity. While all thought of Mankind is still, if not comforted by Grand Narratives, at least caught in representations of a mythological character which it is unable to account for (Creation, human nature and so on), and therefore has, as a last resort in relation to this unthinkable, no other resource than to bring some dogma into play (even if, for example, only to separate mankind from the animal from the point of view of 'essence' – see Schaeffer, 2007, a book I found while proof reading this text and which seems to have a particular affinity with these positions), we now find that the pronouncement of the death of Man, after that of God, finally restores thought to its responsibility (whose witness is Foucault), which even becomes entire. In such an exploration of the human, this agile thought, like Rimbaud's boat, is from that moment without both 'haulers' and ties – without further 'crampons', as Nietzsche said.

It is therefore time to draw out the consequences that follow: the investigation opened up about the diversity of cultures (the *historia* of Herodotus) has from now on ceased to be a mere supplement (or rather a soon-forgotten precedent) to the reflections philosophy has traditionally pursued. It is even far more than a new development of it. For it is henceforth the decisive location for this exploration of the human to be played out. Thus it invites philosophy to emerge from its history for another task. These days it is once more verified: all these patterns of universality, even those which, for their part, have been revealed anew by the cognitive sciences as modules of morality and above all of knowledge, are also always desperately poor. In its reductionism this universal grammar is no more convincing than its formalist precedents. Consequently, for want of being able to support itself on some *given* universality, what other source of information touching upon the human could we utilize than that of a meticulous investigation of all the possible forms tested, and developed in different ways, therefore of the divergence that appears between cultures? Hence this system of self-reflection of the human emerges in which contemporary thought is engaged: the human reflects upon itself (at once mirrors and meditates on itself) in its various relationships. It reveals itself through those of its facets that are illuminated and deployed by multiple cultures as they patiently and intently probe each other: in resistant translation *between* the original languages and their target languages; in the *de-* and *re-*categorization implied in order to pass sideways, without being able to follow the thread of History any longer, as between China and Europe, from one to the other tradition of thought. This word, 'tradition', which has perhaps so little pertinence within a culture, as we recall from Foucault, finds its opportunity in their encounter.

But aren't we led inexorably to the dispersion of the human, people will say in indignation, and therefore to its loss (I can already hear the cry of alarm), if we follow, without further reference to Mankind, these cultural divergences, plunging into the singular, each following its own vein? If there is no longer a 'Mankind' which serves as an anchoring point for this exploration, can the human, torn apart by this diversity, still retain its consistency? You reject what is overarching in Mankind, but do you not then set the human adrift? Under this *dia*, that of divergence and the dialogical, this *auto*, that of self-reflection, itself runs the risk of decomposing . . . *No*, I will say to you, and precisely thanks to the *universal* – at least if it is liberated from all the established universalisms and its power is restored; if, instead of counting as an ideological screed, it effectively serves as a regulatory idea guiding the search. By disclosing all given totality, it will always irrepressibly bring out once again the conditions of possibility for a common that is always threatened by shrinkage and *withdrawal*. And the meaning *of the human* will itself no longer recognize any limits (of fear or of reticence) to its growth and development.

Notes

Itinerary

1   Translators' note: *Communautarisme*. This term is to an extent a French equivalent of 'identity politics', although with a stronger sense of identification, implying that one identifies more strongly with an immediate community than with the greater society and often to the exclusion of other groups.

I   On the universal

1   'The Declaration of 1948 does not state what should be understood by universality' (Fauré, 1988: 21).
2   Translators' note: This phrase, *devoir-être*, presents translation problems throughout the book. It relates to Kantian imperatives as discussed in *Groundwork for the Metaphysics of Morals*, corresponding to the German *sein sollen*.

IV   From the advent of the State to the cosmo-political extension of the common

1   Translators' note: Games organized in commemoration of the death of a great warrior in ancient Greece. See *The Iliad*, Book XXIII, where they are instituted by Achilles in honour of Patroclus.
2   Translators' note: The assembly or market place in the centre of the City where warriors would gather to report for military duty or to hear the pronouncements of the leaders.
3   Translators' note: Erebus: Greek primeval deity, the personification of darkness.
4   See the classical references: Ogereau (2002: 298); Bréhier (2006: 263); Schofield (1991: 64). I thank Jean-François Pradeau for letting me consult his forthcoming article, 'Imiter l'univers, Remarques sur les origines grecques du cosmopolitisme'.
5   Here I agree with Etienne Balibar (1997: 422) in his conclusions about the universal.

V   The other level: the universal as a logical category of philosophy

1   Translators' note: The author is here playing on the closeness of *saveur* and *savoir* in the French language.

VI First encounter of the universal and the common: Roman citizenship extended to the Empire

1 Translators' note: *Immanitas*: brutality, savage character, frightfulness.

VII Paul and the matter of going beyond all communitarianism in Christian universalism

1 I am principally referring here to Bornkamm (1971), as well as the excellent book by Alain Badiou (2003).

VIII Does the question of the universal arise in other cultures?

1 Here I am following the analysis by Erwin Panofsky (1953: 205-46).
2 I would especially like to thank François Déroche for the valuable information he provided me with about this subject.
3 I thank Madeleine Bierdeau and François Chenet in particular for their valuable information about this subject.

IX Are there universal notions? A cultural universal having ideal status

1 'Cultural diversity and transversal values: an East–West dialogue on the dynamic between the spiritual and the temporal', Paris, UNESCO, 7-9 November 2005.
2 To call once more upon Kant (especially on the third *Critique*) in this way so as to unblock what a certain Kantianism itself has jammed up is a path frequently followed in contemporary philosophy (notably in Hannah Arendt); but here I propose to transfer the approach to the dialogue of cultures, which is a fresh stake.

X On human rights – the notion of universalizing

1 In deliberations conducted over more than twenty years, Marcel Gauchet has shown that human rights 'could not be a political policy', then that, if they had become one, it was the price of an ideological consensualization which had led to the eclipse of the political that we acknowledge today (see the articles from *Débat* from July to August 1980 and from May to August 2000, reprinted in Gauchet, 2002: 1-26, 326-85). While being fully in agreement with these analyses, I can only observe that the question of human rights has sprung up once again today due to the fact that it gives form to (and serves as a faultline in) the open conflict between cultures: it is therefore also to be considered on this level which puts the conception of the universal directly at stake.

2 This is the argument for 'Harmony' which is in fact systematically invoked today by Chinese leaders so as to thwart the Western postulation of human rights as well as the denunciation that Westerners make of their violation in China. As I write this in 2008, it can easily be noted in the Chinese press over recent months how the Olympic Games was at first refused to Beijing in the name of human rights, but was accorded for 2008 under the pressure of economic interests and their political realism, making clear this conflict of values.

3 With an agile pen, Marcel Gauchet has analysed perfectly how, through its 'evangelical simplicity' and by benefiting from a new confusion between the intellectual sphere and that of the media, the credo of human rights offered itself a clear conscience at a bargain price: its consensual ideology is all the more welcome in that it cultivates an oppositional posture and makes do with the evidence of the scandalous. Hence, the comfort of a position which willingly and brilliantly lays into all reflection about them: for would 'seeking to know, seeking to understand' not necessarily mean 'wanting to defer faced with the urgency of what is intolerable', 'to begin to come to terms with the unacceptable', 'to seek excuses for the inexcusable'? . . . (Gauchet, 2002: 357). It is especially verifiable, when it comes to China, how it is our once hardline revolutionaries who, 'as prudent tacticians', in fact, have committed themselves to a new career by substituting human rights for their earlier dogmatism.

4 See, for example, Donnelly, 2007: ch. 3, 'The Relative Universality of Human Rights'.

5 If I believe it is necessary to describe this unconditional, and therefore absolute, dimension of human rights in terms of a *negative* dimension (it is the deprivation or want of human rights which opens, at the very heart of experience, onto an unconditional quality of experience and consequently sustains a legitimate *a-priori* refusal), it is because this cannot be done, it seems to me, in terms of a *minimum*, as is ordinarily the case, or more precisely as a 'minimal pragmatic point allowing very diverse people to gather in a struggle against dictatorships, despotisms, tyrannies and totalitarianisms of all types which flourish on the planet' (Gauchet, 2002: 2-3). For then how precisely should this 'minimum' be fixed in a transcultural way, one which would not necessarily have to be relative?

6 Translators' note: This is another Kantian reference, in German *sein Können*.

XI From where is the common derived if it is neither synthesis, denominator nor foundation?

1 On this naive conception of a radical alterity calling for a felicitous complementarity between the West and China, see Ryckmans, 2006: 6.

2 See, for example, the position of Sebastiano Maffetone in Latour and Gagliardi (2006: 89ff.)

3 Chosen at random, let's mention the general Conference of Unesco, 33rd session, Paris 2005, 'Celebration of an international year of global consciousness and the

ethics of dialogue among peoples'; or the 'Medium-Term Strategy' project of 2008-13 (34C/4) ('Overarching objective 4/10: Demonstrating the importance of exchange and dialogue among cultures for social cohesion and reconciliation in order to develop a culture of peace'), or the publication by Bindé et al. (1999: 470ff.) – pages that express nothing but self-righteousness.

4 Translators' note: Even more difficult in English, in which 'esprit' translates as both 'mind' and 'spirit'.

5 Translators' note: This last phrase is translated from the French as the English translation (which follows) seems to bear only a distant relation to the French: 'he [the sceptic] has dropped out of communicative action, even as a thought experiment'.

XII On 'Cultures': divergences of language – the resources of thought

1 'All we wish to show here is that *the linguistic structure of Greek predisposed* the notion of "being" to a philosophical vocation' (Benveniste, 1971: 63; emphasis added).

XIII Constructing the dialogue between cultures to counter the surrounding uniformization; human self-reflection

1 I have to wonder: how can we hope to 'have done' with alterity in philosophy, when it is evidently (haven't we known this since Plato?) one of its principal concepts?

2 Such a persistence in this stubborn opposition is that of Jean-Luc Domenach (2008: 180ff.).

Bibliography

[Translators' note. In accordance with the wishes of the author, translations of classical works throughout the text have generally been made from the French rather than from existing translations. We have, however, checked our translations and made use of the editions cited in the bibliography.]

Abu-Salieh, Sami A. Aldeeb (1994) *Les Musulmans face aux droits de l'homme: religion & droit & politique: étude et documents*. Bochum: D. Winkler.

Apel, Karl-Otto (1981) 'La question d'une fondation ultime de la raison', translated into French by Suzanne Foisy and Jacques Poulain, *Critique*, 413, October (German original 'Die Situation des Menschen als ethisches Problem' in (1988) *Diskurs und Verantwortung*. Frankfurt am Main: Suhrkamp).

Apel, Karl-Otto (1988) 'La rationalité de la communication humaine dans la perspective de la pragmatique transcendentale', translated into French by Jean-Michel de Lannou, *Critique*, 493-4, June–July (German original 'Die transzendentalpragmatische Begründung der Kommunikationsethik und das Problem der höchsten Stufe einer Entwicklungslogik des moralischen Bewußtseins' in (1988) *Diskurs und Verantwortung*. Frankfurt am Main: Suhrkamp).

Aristotle (1984) *Metaphysics* in *The Complete Works of Aristotle*, edited and translated by Jonathan Barnes. Princeton, NJ: Princeton University Press.

Augustine, Saint, Bishop of Hippo (1962) *My Confessions*, translated by E. B. Pusey. London: Dent, Everyman Library.

Badiou, Alain (2003) *Saint Paul: The Foundation of Universalism*, translated by Ray Brassier. Stanford, Calif: Stanford University Press.

Balibar, Etienne (1997) *La crainte des masses*. Paris: Galilée.

Barnes, Jonathan (1979) *The Presocratic Philosophers*. Vol. II, *Empedocles to Democritus*. London: Routledge and Kegan Paul.

Benveniste, Emile (1971) *Problems of General Linguistics*, translated by Mary Elizabeth Meek, 2 vols. Coral Gables, Fla.: University of Miami Press.

Biardeau, Madeleine (1964) *Théorie de la connaissance et philosophie de la parole dans le Brahmanisme classique*. Paris: Editions de l'Ecole des Hautes Etudes en Sciences Sociales.

Billeter, Jean-François (2006) *Contre François Jullien*. Paris: Allia.

Bornkamm, Gunther (1971) *Paul*, translated from the German by D. M. G. Stalker. New York: Harper and Row; London: Hodder and Stoughton.

Bossuet, Jacques-Benigne (1976) *Discourse on Universal History*. Chicago: University of Chicago Press.

Brague, Rémi (1992) *Europe, la voie romaine*. Paris: Criterion.

Braque, Georges (1952) *Le jour et la nuit*. Paris: Gallimard.

Bréhier, Emile (2006) *Chrysippe et l'ancien stoïcisme*. Paris: Archives Contemporaines Editions.

Bibliography

Cheng, Anne Anlin (2007) 'Pour en finir avec le mythe de l'alterité' in *La pensée en Chine aujourd'hui*, under the direction of Anne Cheng. Paris: Gallimard.

Cicero, Marcus Tullius (1913) *De officiis*, translated by Walter Miller. Cambridge, Mass.: Harvard University Press; London: Heinemann.

Cicero, Marcus Tullius (2001) *The Ideal Orator (De Oratore)*, translated by J. M. May and J. Wisse. Oxford: Oxford University Press.

Confucius (1993) *The Analects*, translated with an introduction and notes by Raymond Dawson. Oxford and New York: Oxford University Press.

Delmas-Marty, Mireille (2007) *Towards a Truly Common Law: Europe as a Laboratory for Legal Pluralism*, translated by Naomi Norberg. Cambridge: Cambridge University Press.

Descartes, René (1996) *Meditations on First Philosophy: With Selections from the Objections and Replies*, translated and edited by John Cottingham with an introductory essay by Bernard Williams. Cambridge: Cambridge University Press.

Descola, Philippe (2005) *Par-delà nature et culture*. Paris: Editions Gallimard.

Detienne, Marcel (1999) *The Masters of Truth in Archaic Greece*, translated by Janet Lloyd and Pierre Vidal-Naquet. Cambride, Mass.: Zone.

Diogenes Laertius (1853) *The Lives and Opinions of Eminent Philosophers*, translated by C.D. Yonge. London: Henry G. Bohn.

Domenach, Jean-Luc (2008) 'Coup de sonde', *Esprit*, 6.

Donnelly, Jack (2007) *International Human Rights*. Boulder, Colo.: Westview Press.

Dravid, Raja Ram (2001) *The Problem of Universals in Indian Philosophy*. Delhi: Motilal Banarsidass Publishers.

Eberhard, Christophe (1999) 'Pluralisme et dialogisme: les droits de l'homme dans un mondialisation qui ne soit pas seulement une occidentalisation' in *Le retour de l'ethnocentrisme: purification ethnique versus universalisme cannibale* (Revue du MAUSS 13). Paris: La Découverte.

Esposito, Roberto (2009) *Communitas: The Origin and Destiny of Community (Cultural Memory in the Present)*, translated by Timothy Campbell. Palo Alto, Calif.: Stanford University Press.

Fauré, Christine (ed.) (1988) *Les Déclarations des droits de l'homme de 1789*. Paris: Payot.

Gauchet, Marcel (1989) *La révolution des droits de l'homme*. Paris: Gallimard.

Gauchet, Marcel (2002) *La démocratie contre elle-même*. Paris: Gallimard.

Guo Qingfan (n.d.) *Xiaozheng Zhuangzi jishi*. Taipei: Shijie shuju.

Habermas, Jürgen (1983) *Moralbewusstsein und kommunikatives Handeln*. Frankfurt am Main: Suhrkampf.

Habermas, Jürgen (2001) *Moral Consciousness and Communicative Action*, translated by Shierry Weber Nicholsen and Christian Lenhardt. Cambridge, Mass.: MIT Press.

Hegel, Georg Wilhelm Friedrich (1953) *Reason in History: A General Introduction to the Philosophy of History*, translated by Robert S. Hartman. New York: Liberal Arts Press.

Hegel, Georg Wilhelm Friedrich (1977) *Phenomenology of Spirit*, translated by A.V. Miller with analysis of the text and foreword by J. N. Findlay. Oxford: Clarendon Press.

Hegel, Georg Wilhelm Friedrich (2006) *Lectures on the History of Philosophy*; edited by

Robert F. Brown and translated by R. F. Brown and J. M. Stewart with the assistance of H. S. Harris. Oxford and New York: Oxford University Press.

Heraclitus, of Ephesus (1979) *The Art and Thought of Heraclitus: An Edition of the Fragments*, translated by Charles H. Kahn. Cambridge: Cambridge University Press.

Heraclitus, of Ephesus (1994) *Fragments*, translated by Dennis Sweet. Lanham, Md. and London: University Press of America.

Herodotus (1997) *The Histories*, translated by Robin Waterfield with an Introduction and notes by Carolyn Dewald. Oxford: Oxford University Press.

Hersch, Jeanne (1999) 'Les fondements des droits de l'homme dans la conscience universelle' in *La Déclaration universelle des droits de l'homme, 1948-98: Avenir d'un ideal commun. Actes du colloque des 14, 15 et 16 septembre 1998 à la Sorbonne, Paris*. Paris: La Documentation française.

Hobbes, Thomas (1997) *Leviathan*, edited by Richard E. Flathman and David Johnston. New York and London: W. W. Norton.

Huntington, Samuel P. (1996) *The Clash of Civilizations and the Remaking of World Order*. New York: Simon & Schuster.

Irenaeus of Lyons (2010) *Against Heresies*, edited by Alexander Roberts, James Donaldson and A. Cleveland Coxe. CreateSpace.

Jullien, François (1998) *Un Sage est sans idée*. Paris: Seuil.

Jullien, François (2000) *Penser d'un dehors (la Chine)*. Paris: Seuil.

Jullien, François (2001) *Du 'Temps', éléments d'une philosophie du vivre*. Paris: Grasset.

Jullien, François (2003) *La grande image n'a pas de forme*. Paris: Grasset.

Jullien, François (2004) *L'ombre au tableau, Du mal ou du négatif*. Paris: Seuil.

Jullien, François (2005) *Nourrir sa vie, à l'écart du bonheur*. Paris: Seuil.

Jullien, François (2006) *Si parler va sans dire. Du* logos *et autres ressources*. Paris: Seuil.

Jullien, François (2007) *Chemin faisant, connaître la Chine, relancer la philosophie*. Paris: Seuil.

Kahn, Charles H. (1973) *The Verb 'Be' in Ancient Greece*. Dordrecht and Boston: D. Reidel.

Kant, Immanuel (1969) *Foundations of the Metaphysics of Morals*, translated by Lewis White Beck, with critical essays edited by Robert Paul Wolff. New York: Macmillan; London: Collier Macmillan.

Kant, Immanuel (1978) *The Critique of Judgement*, translated with analytical indexes by James Creed Meredith. Oxford: Clarendon Press.

Kant, Immanuel (2003) *Critique of Pure Reason*, translated by Norman Kemp Smith, with a new introduction by Howard Caygill. Basingstoke: Palgrave Macmillan.

Küng, Hans, and Karl-Josef Kuschel (1997) *Global Ethic: The Declaration of the Parliament of the World's Religions*. New York: Continuum.

Laclau, Ernesto (1999) 'L'universalisme, le particularisme et la question de l'identité' in *Le retour de l'ethnocentrisme: purification ethnique versus universalisme cannibale* (Revue du MAUSS 13). Paris: La Découverte.

Lao-tzeu (1967) *Tao tö king*, translated by Liou Kia-hway. Paris: Gallimard.

Lao-tzeu (2009) *La Voie et sa vertu*, translated by Pierre Leyris and François Houang. Paris: Seuil.

Latour, Bruno, and Pascale Gagliardi (eds.) (2006) *Les atmosphères de la politique. Dialogue pour un monde commun.* Paris: Les Empêcheurs de penser en rond.

Libera, Alain de (1996) *La querelle des universaux – de Platon à la fin du Moyen-Age.* Paris: Seuil.

Marcus Aurelius (1944) *The Meditations*, edited with translation and commentary by A. S. L. Farquharson. Oxford: Clarendon.

Marx, Karl (1975) *On the Jewish Question* in *Early Writings*, translated by Gregor Benton. Harmondsworth: Penguin.

Mayor, Federico, with Jérôme Bindé, Jean-Yves Le Saux and Ragnar Gudmundsson (1999) *Un monde nouveau.* UNESCO / Odile Jacob.

Mencius (1963) translated with notes by W. A. C. H. Dobson. London: Oxford University Press.

Mencius (1998) translated by David Hinton. Washington, DC: Counterpoint.

Moatti, Claudia (1997) *Raison de Rome.* Paris: Seuil.

Nietzsche, Friedrich (1966) *Beyond Good and Evil: Prelude to a Philosophy of the Future*, translated with commentary by Walter Kaufmann. New York: Random House.

Ogereau, F. (2002) *Essai sur le système philosophique des stoïciens.* Paris: Encre Marine.

Panniker, Raimundo (1998) 'La notion des droits de l'homme est-elle un concept occidental?' in *Le retour de l'ethnocentrisme: purification ethnique versus universalisme cannibale* (Revue du MAUSS 13). Paris: La Découverte.

Panofsky, Erwin (1953) *Early Netherlandish Painting: Its Origins and Character*, 2 vols. Cambridge, Mass.: Harvard University Press.

Pliny, the Elder (1952) *Natural History*, Vol. X, with an English translation in ten volumes by H. Rackham. London: Heinemann; Cambridge, Mass.: Harvard University Press.

Quintilian (1920-2) *Institutio Oratoria*, translated by H. E. Butler (Loeb Classical Library). London: Heinemann.

Ryckmans, Pierre (Simon Leys) (2006) 'Connaître et méconnaître la Chine', *Le Magazine Littéraire*, 455, July–August.

Schaeffer, Jean-Marie (2007) *La fin de l'exception humaine.* Paris: Editions Gallimard.

Schofield, Malcolm (1991) *The Stoic Idea of the City.* Cambridge: Cambridge University Press.

Seneca, Lucius Annaeus (2011) *On Benefits*, translated by Miriam Griffin and Brad Inwood. Chicago, Ill. and London: University of Chicago Press.

Stobaei, Joannis (1822) *Florilegium, ad manuscriptorum fidem emendavit et supplevit Thomas Gaisford*, 4 vols. Oxford.

Thomas, Yan (1996) '"Origine" et "commune patrie": étude de droit public romain (89 av. J.-C. – 212 apr. J.-C.)', *Bulletin de l'École Française de Rome*, 221.

UNESCO International Conference (2005) 'Diversité culturelle et valeurs transversales: un dialogue Est–Ouest sur le dynamique entre le spirituel et le temporel', Paris, UNESCO, 7-9 November.

Unger, Ulrich (2003) 'Goldene Regel und Konfuzianismus', *Minima sinica*, 2.

Terence (1988) *The Self-tormentor*, edited with translation and commentary by A. J. Brothers. Warminster: Aris & Phillips.

Vadet, Jean-Claude (1995) *Les idées morales dans l'Islam.* Paris: Presses universitaires de France.

Villey, Michel (1986) *Le droit et les droits de l'homme*. Paris: Presses universitaires de France.

Wu Kuang-ming (1998) 'Time in China' in *On the 'Logic' of Togetherness, a Cultural Hermeneutic*. Leiden: Brill.

Zhang Yinde (2007) '"La sinité": l'identité chinoise en question' in *La pensée en Chine aujourd'hui*, under the direction of Anne Cheng. Paris: Gallimard.

Index